PRAISE FOR THE BOOK

'This book is certainly a masterpiece. It will help you to master your memory.'

Dr Biswaroop Roy Chowdhury
Chief Editor, Asia Book of Records

'I have known Aditi since the last 4–5 years when she wanted to make it to the *Limca Book of Records* for the fastest calculation. Not only did she make that record, she went on gathering laurels culminating with the Guinness World Record! Since then Aditi and her husband Sudhir have become well-known for memory techniques, holding memory sessions and workshops. In fact, often I seek her advice to solve a record issue. The section on specific subjects like Biology, Chemistry etc. will be a boon book for students. I wish Aditi and Sudhir all the best for their book *How to Memorize Anything,* a book which will help thousands to be memory perfect!'

Vijaya Ghose
Editor, Limca Book of Records

The book *How to Memorize Anything* focuses on fundamentals of memory techniques to improve memory, bringing about a better understanding of the brain, using the right software for garnering and nurturing potential of the mind, and has a separate subject-wise section for students. Knowing Aditi and Sudhir as I do, this book will create great impact in pushing the mental boundaries into unexplored regions.'

Syed Samar Hamid
Additional Secretary, Hamdard Education Society

'Using these techniques, I can now memorize my answers, formulae, and vocabulary effectively and efficiently. It helped me improve my life as well.'

Koyal Rana
Miss India World, 2014
(Learnt memory techniques from us in the 12th standard)

'I am glad that Aditi and Sudhir have come up with a book that makes important contribution to this important field of study. The book is written in a very simple language accessible to laymen without much scientific jargon. I am sure this book will inspire students and professionals alike to focus and sharpen their memory using myriad techniques listed in the book.'

Bala Kishore
Senior Vice President, United Online Software Development
(India) Pvt. Ltd., Hyderabad

'A logically compiled combination of facts, literature survey and applied research on memory function useful for students and entrepreneurs alike. On the one hand the book is written using words easily comprehensible by those whose native language is not English, and on the other hand, it covers the topic exhaustively. I have used memory skills described in the book and found them very useful, especially mind maps, to improve my memory.'

Dr Mitrabasu
Sc F, Joint Director and Head, Clinical and Allied Operations
Management, INMAS, DRDO

'Memory training has changed my life. I use them every single day—I love it! Now I learn any subject ten times faster than ever before. These techniques helped me to make 9 world records and 6 national records. This book will certainly help many others to make records like me.'

Dr Himmat Bhardwaj
(Holder of numerous memory records)

'Memory techniques taught in this book are wonderful with miraculous results. They not only improve my ability to retain facts and data but also made recall very quick.'

Bharat Bhushan
IES, Financial Advisor,
Bhakra Beas Management Board, Chandigarh

'Learning memory techniques was a great experience for both my children; one is in grade 8 and the second one is in grade 3. Learning long list of items, associating numbers with symbols, cramming up names of states, Countries and capitals was all so difficult and never ending until they learnt the wonderful memory techniques which made learning more easier and logical. Thank you Aditi and Sudhir for giving both my children the gift that you have worked so hard for. I have taken certain tips from them and I am using them myself to remember my own presentations. This book will be a boon for students as well as people from all walks of life.'

Parul Jain
Mother of Vridhi Jain,
8th Class, Modern School, Barakhamba Road

HOW TO
MEMORIZE
ANYTHING

HOW TO
MEMORIZE
ANYTHING

THE ULTIMATE HANDBOOK TO EXPLORE
AND IMPROVE YOUR MEMORY

ADITI SINGHAL
SUDHIR SINGHAL

RANDOM HOUSE INDIA

Published by Random House India in 2015

1

Copyright © Aditi Singhal, Sudhir Singhal 2015

Illustrations © Aditi Singhal and Sudhir Singhal

Random House Publishers India Private Limited
7th Floor, Infinity Tower C, DLF Cyber City
Gurgaon–122 002
Haryana, India

Random House Group Limited
20 Vauxhall Bridge Road
London SW1V 2SA
United Kingdom

978 81 8400 521 9

Any advice in terms of supplements, generic ingredients of cosmeceuticals, or any mention of a trade name in the book should be taken only upon your doctor's recommendation.

Illustrations credit: M. Saquib

Typeset in Adobe Garamond by Saanvi Graphics, Noida

Printed and bound in India by Replika Press Private Limited

A PENGUIN RANDOM HOUSE COMPANY

To the

Almighty God,

the supreme father of all souls and the source of true knowledge.

Contents

PART B: MEMORY TECHNIQUES AND THEIR APPLICATIONS

PART C: STUDENT SECTION

PART D: TRICKS TO AMAZE YOUR FRIENDS

PREFACE

As memory trainers, we conduct numerous seminars and workshops in a number of organizations across the country throughout the year. During such seminars, when we perform some challenging memory exercises *(like memorizing number sequences, words, etc.)*, the immediate expression we see on the faces of our audience is of disbelief and amazement. They all wonder how we can have such an outstanding photographic memory.

We are often asked, *'Is it God gifted?'* Sometimes people even ask us to sprinkle some magical memory power on them too. And we tell them that there is nothing magical in it. In fact, anyone can have a good memory if you know the right tricks.

They actually don't believe us when we tell them this and the next question they ask is: 'Do you mean we can have one too?' 'Is it really possible?' And smilingly we assure them, *'YES! It is possible.'*

In fact, the good news is that we can all have a very sharp memory as we've all been gifted with a wonderful machine called the **'BRAIN'** which has the capacity to store infinite information and this capacity is almost the same for everyone. All of us have the same kind of hardware, i.e. brain structure, but the difference lies in the software we use to operate it. By 'software', we mean the right knowledge to use our brain and memory. And many a times, during our workshops in schools for children, we assure them that once they also download this software, they'll be able to memorize things faster than us. How?? The answer is very simple—students use the latest hardware and just need to know how to **download** and use the right software.

I, Aditi Singhal, can confidently say, from my personal experience, that any-body can do this. Five years back, I was a worried housewife who believed that my memory was fading day-by-day. I would forget to check milk after putting it to boil or forget to keep back the jewellery that I had worn to a party a night before or forget to make important phone calls or miss important appointments. Believe me, I was having a tough time as everyone in my family started complaining about my failing memory. I even considered consulting a doctor about this problem as I thought it was turning serious. Then one day I happened to attend a seminar on memory by renowned memory trainer Dr Biswaroop Roy Chaudhary. That program was an eye opener for me. I got to know many interesting facts about the human memory and brain. The session inspired me to further explore human memory and techniques to improve it. I started reading many books and attended some more seminars about it. I was determined to improve my memory and started using the techniques practically in my daily routine work.

Once I realized the difference it made in my life, I started sharing this knowledge with a few students with an aim to help them memorize their course content. One day when I was teaching 9th class students how to memorize a chemistry periodic table, my son Devansh, who was just 5-years-old at that time, showed keenness to participate in the session as well. To my utter surprise, he could memorize 10 elements from the periodic table in just 5 minutes. He insisted on learning more and within a week he had achieved the accomplishment for being **the *youngest Indian to memorize the complete periodic table*** and his name was registered in the *India Book of Records*. It was unbelievable but true. I felt proud every time I saw articles on Devansh's achievements in leading newspapers and magazines.

Motivated by his performance, I started teaching these techniques to people from all walks of life, especially students and teachers. The response was very positive and very soon, many of my students also made numerous National and World Records and the *India Book of Records* awarded me with the title of 'Best Memory Trainer'.

I also went on to make two National Records for 'fastest calculation' and 'memorizing binary numbers' awarded by the *Limca Book of Records*.

Using these wonderful memory techniques, we broke another record in the *Guinness World Records* for 'conducting the largest Math class', helping 2,312 students memorize tables till 99.

The journey from a homemaker to a World Record holder seems like a dream come true. It also proves that anybody who is interested in improving his or her memory can do so.

Seeing the overwhelming response from readers of my first book *How to Become a Human Calculator?*—how it is helping them get rid of Maths phobia, regenerating their interest in the subject, and developing self-confidence about their own calculation skills— my husband, Sudhir Singhal, who himself is a trainer and very passionate about these techniques, motivated me to share these wonderful, life-changing techniques with people all over the world by writing another book on tech-niques to improve your memory.

Our vision is to spread this awareness among people around the globe that we all have the same brain potential to memorize anything and everything, provided we know how to use it.

This book will serve as an instruction manual to help you understand your brain better and help you *download* the required software to harness its maximum potential, hence improving your memory.

Reading this book is smart. Putting what you learn into practice is even smarter.

So what are we waiting for? Let's get started!

Aditi Singhal
(mvedica@gmail.com)
(www.aditisinghal.com)

SELF ASSESSMENT

HOW GOOD IS YOUR MEMORY?

Before we begin the journey of improving your memory, it is first necessary to assess your present memory level. Only when you have a clear picture of where you are now, will you be able to start moving towards where you would like to be.

TEST #1:

Answer 'yes' or 'no' to the following statements:

1.	Do you ever go into a room and forget what you went in for?	Yes	No
2.	Do you have difficulty recalling passwords and PINs?	Yes	No
3.	Do you exercise to keep your brain active?	Yes	No
4.	Do you misplace your keys/mobile phone often?	Yes	No
5.	Do you always remember your friends' and relatives' birthdays?	Yes	No

6.	Do you have difficulty remembering people's names or phone numbers?	Yes	No
7.	Do you keep yourself organized?	Yes	No
8.	Do you often forget to purchase necessary items from the market?	Yes	No
9.	Do you find it difficult to learn new words and their meanings?	Yes	No
10.	Do you sometimes forget to lock the door of your house or car and repeatedly need to check it as you go out?	Yes	No
11.	Do you often forget your papers/notebooks or bag in office or at a friend's house?	Yes	No
12.	Do you often get stuck in the middle of an examination or forget a speech halfway?	Yes	No

Scoring: For every 'NO', you score 1 point or else 0.
Your score: _____

TEST #2:

Time allowed: For Memorizing: 3 minutes, for Recalling: 5 minutes
You get 3 minutes to memorize the following 30-digit number. After your time is up, turn to the Recall Sheet (given on the next page) and try to write down this number within 5 minutes.

243946102834892997834167204578

Scoring: For every digit recalled correctly in sequence, you score 1 point.

TEST #3:

Time allowed: Memorizing 5 minutes, Recalling 8 minutes

Here is a list of numbered items. Take about 5 minutes to memorize the twenty items listed here, by number. You must remember not only the item, but to which number it belongs.

After 5 minutes turn to the Recall Sheet on the next page where these numbers will be jumbled, and you will be asked to recall the word corresponding to each number from 1 to 20 within 8 minutes.

1	Wood	11	Flowers
2	Pen	12	Snake
3	Car	13	Gift
4	Window	14	Bag
5	Jacket	15	Monitor
6	Book	16	Shoes
7	Mango	17	Table
8	Mobile	18	Paper
9	Speakers	19	Clothes
10	Mirror	20	Carpet

Scoring: For every word recalled correctly, you score 1 point.

RECALL SHEET

Test #2

Recall time: 5 minutes

Scoring: For every digit entered correctly in the right sequence, you score 1 point.

Your score: _____

Test #3

Recall time: 8 minutes
   Scoring: For every word written correctly, you score 1 point.

16		9	
5		15	
12		10	
6		14	
8		5	
1		3	
18		7	
13		17	
2		11	
19		4	

Your score: _____

Performance Analysis

So how was your overall performance? To find out, fill the following chart:

Test No.	Your Score
Test #1	
Test #2	
Test #3	
Total score	_____

IF YOUR SCORE IS BETWEEN 1 TO 25

You need to work on the fundamentals of memory. Pay special attention to the first section of this book and you will see a dramatic improvement in no time.

IF YOUR SCORE IS BETWEEN 26 TO 49

You are already using a few of the memory techniques (knowingly or unknowingly). This book will help you in further improving and enhancing your memory skills.

IF YOUR SCORE IS BETWEEN 50 TO 62

You are using your memory very efficiently. Have a look at the table of contents and focus on the areas where you need to do some fine-tuning to really unleash your true potential.

This book contains a lot of techniques and methods that will enable the reader to drastically improve his/her level of memorizing things. After learning techniques from this book, you can perform these tests again and see the difference.

So, let's embark on the journey of memory with a belief to bring about a change!

WHY MEMORY TRAINING?

Imagine purchasing the most expensive car in the world, but if you don't know how to drive it, what's the use of purchasing it? Similarly, we all know that the human brain works faster than the fastest computer in the world, but it is not enough to simply be aware of the potential of the human brain. One should also know how to use it to the optimum.

Similarly, in schools and colleges we have always been bombarded with loads of information, but have we ever been told *how to store this information in our brain*? Students are being taught different subjects, like Mathematics, Science, Computers, etc. but they miss a very important subject, i.e. the **brain**, with the help of which we can learn other subjects. *Were you ever taught how to use this computer?*

When you purchase any home appliance, like a washing machine, a microwave, or say a computer for the first time, how do you get to know how to use it? You learn through reading its instruction manual or getting a trainer to demonstrate it. Similarly, God has given each one of us a living computer more powerful and faster than anything created in any factory, i.e, our brain. However, God didn't give us a formal instruction manual for this powerful and wonderful machine.

This book is an effort to serve you as an instruction manual of this brain. It will enable you to first understand its mechanism and then to use it more effectively.

WHAT ARE THE BENEFITS OF TRAINED MEMORY?

A good memory is a powerful asset in everyone's life—whether you're a student, an executive, a homemaker, or a businessman. The better your memory, the better are your chances of excelling in your respective fields.

For students

If you are a student, think how wonderful it would be if you could remember everything that is taught in the class and recall it efficiently during the examinations.

For parents

If parents have the knowledge of how to train their memory, they can guide their children to do better in school right from their childhood. Their own memory will improve dramatically by doing so, which in turn will help them in their business or profession.

For homemakers

If you are a homemaker, imagine the euphoria of remembering all details of household expenses, bills, amount paid, shopping lists, prices of different items purchased, etc.

For teachers

You can become your students' favourite teacher by helping them to remember their subject using memory techniques.

For business people

Business people may ask, 'What's the use of memory techniques for us when we have computers and secretaries to help us out?' But think of all the benefits of having names and faces of all your clients and your business transactions at your fingertips. An accurate and retentive memory is the basis of all business success.

For marketing executives

Can you imagine the impression you can make on your boss if you were to reel out all the sales figures at a moment's notice?

For professionals

- ❖ A doctor is almost always required to diagnose and treat a patient without having to refer to the book.
- ❖ Lawyers too have to remember all the laws given in law books. All the acts required for the cases are available in innumerable books. But the lawyer needs to remember all relevant laws while representing the case.
- ❖ Authors, psychiatrists, computer engineers, and all other professionals also have to remember a lot of relevant information in their particular fields.

So, no matter what your age or profession, a good memory is important for everyone. Let's start the journey of training our memory by understanding it first and then learning the techniques and methods to use it to its optimum.

PART A

BASICS OF MEMORY

1

UNDERSTANDING MEMORY

How many times have you misplaced your keys and wasted all your time looking for them?

How often have you gone to your room and opened the cupboard to take out something only to find yourself standing there wondering *why have you opened it?* And once you go back to the other room and resume your work, that's when you recall what you wanted.

How often do you find yourself in an embarrassing situation where you happen to meet someone in the market who is known to you but you cannot recall the person's name? It's only later, when you are busy in some other work, that the name pops up in your head.

Things get worse when it comes to studies. I am sure as a student you too must have faced situations where, even after preparing well for an exam and revising the course in the morning, you forget everything as soon as you get the question paper in your hand. And the amazing part is that when you leave the examination hall, most of the answers come back to you  and you suddenly remember everything. The result is low scores even after working extremely hard.

After such incidences, you might feel that you have a poor memory and may be concerned about improving it. Well, one of the best ways to try to improve it is to understand more about its nature and how it works.

WHAT IS MEMORY?

Memory is the process by which information about the world is stored in our brain in order to give us a sense of who we are. It tells us what we did yesterday or five years ago and it guides us on what to do tomorrow. Memories of our childhood may be triggered by a nursery rhyme or a romantic memory may come to mind when we listen to a particular song. Just imagine, what would happen if you suddenly lose your memory? Just stop and imagine for 2 minutes! You would be good for nothing. As *Plato* said about memory—'*All knowledge is but remembrance*'. If you lose your memory completely, you would have to start learning everything from scratch, just like a newborn baby.

In fact, whatever we do in our life every second can be attributed to memory as all our knowledge is based on it. An example to support this: You would not be able to read this book right now if you didn't remember the sounds of the 26 letters of the alphabet.

POTENTIAL OF HUMAN MEMORY

The human brain consists of about 100 billion neurons. Each neuron forms about 1,000 connections with other neurons, amounting to more than a trillion connections, each connection helping with many memories at a time, exponentially increasing the brain's memory storage capacity to something closer to around 2.5 petabytes (or a million gigabytes).

For comparison, if your brain worked like a digital video recorder in a television, 2.5 petabytes would be enough to hold 3 million hours of TV shows. You would have to leave the TV running continuously for more than 300 years to use up all that storage. That means, we don't have to worry about running out of space in our lifetime.

But the reality is that most of us are unaware of the potential of the brain and its capacity to store information, and the right way to use that. Due to this we are not able to harness its real potential and with time and experience develop wrong beliefs about our own memory.

SOME MYTHS ABOUT MEMORY

MYTH: Our memory will be full if we try to remember more

FACT: There is no limit to the capacity of memory. Most people believe that trying to remember too much would be very confusing. Rather, researchers have shown that memory is like a muscle. Just like muscle needs to be exercised and developed in order to increase stamina, in the same way memory can be developed using special memory skills whereby you can use

already remembered data as a tool to remember new data which further serves as a tool for some other new data thus increasing your memory exponentially. The fact is **the more you remember, the more you CAN remember.**

MYTH: My memory is failing due to age

FACT: As mentioned earlier, memory is like a muscle—*use it or lose it*. It is true neurons deplete with age. But recent studies show that we can actually develop new cells throughout our life provided we keep exercising our brain. Like our body can be kept fit in old age, similarly we can be mentally fit as well. Researchers suggest that new experiences and learning new information are key to  memory improvement exercises. So, using memory skills, an elderly person can memorize better than a 20-year-old person who is not using any such skills.

MYTH: Pills can help me improve my memory

FACT: Pills and tonics can be effective but in a very limited way. These pills may help you to have a healthy brain by providing some necessary vitamins and minerals required by the brain to function efficiently, but a healthy brain does not guarantee a good memory. You might be having a healthy body but that does not assure that you are a good athlete; for that you need to be trained.  Similarly, the easiest way to improve your memory is to learn memory techniques.

MYTH: Different people have different memory capacity

FACT: Each one of us has the same hardware, i.e. *Brain*, with almost the same mass, size, neurons, as far as built-up is concerned. So the difference in the working of memory of different people lies in the **utilization levels** and *not in the built-in capacities*.

WE ARE ALL EQUAL!

Think of a company, where there are 100 people with 1 computer each, having the same configuration. Yet each individual makes use of that computer according to his/her need and knowledge of using it.

Today, everybody is using a Smartphone with multiple functions and applications. But some people use it only to update their *Facebook* status or socialize on *WhatsApp*, while others only to make or receive a call. At the same time, there are many people who use all the features of the phone which help them in their day to day life like *checking e-mails, handling financial matters, making presentation while on the go, etc*, thus making the best use of their time and the gadget.

Some people might have better brain power than others because of heredity, lifestyle, and the nutrition they get in their growing years, etc. Yet, memory is not a finite entity, inherited genetically and fixed at birth. **It can be trained and developed**.

HOW ARE MEMORIES FORMED? *(3 Rs OF MEMORY)*

After doing a lot of research on memory, scientists have suggested that the process of memorizing can be divided into 3 main stages:

1. **Registration:** taking in information

2. **Retention**: storing information
3. **Recollection**: retrieving information from our stores as and when required

It can be compared with a computer where the three steps are input, storage, and output of data.

How are the 3 Rs important?

1. REGISTRATION: Input of information through five senses is the first step in the formation of any memory. The data is then filed in the short-term memory system, which is very limited. At this stage the sense organs have to be alert enough to be able to register the information clearly. Otherwise, the waste and negative thoughts coming from the subconscious mind might replace it soon. If the registration is good, the memory formed will also be stronger.

THE MYSTERIOUS CASE OF THE MISSING KEYS

Rohit turns the key in the doorknob to open the door of his house and switches on the lights, while simultaneously talking on his mobile. He closes the door behind him, reaches the kitchen, put the keys on the kitchen shelf, takes a glass of water from the refrigerator, comes to his bedroom, loosens his tie, and makes himself comfortable on the couch. After 2 more minutes of conversation, he ends the call and goes to the other room to unlock it. But he finds that the keys are missing. He keeps on searching for the keys in frustration for 10 minutes till he finds them in the kitchen. He is amazed how could he forget where he kept the keys just a few minutes back!

Don't we all often find ourselves in a situation similar to Rohit? Now let's try to comprehend what happened with him. When he entered the kitchen and kept the keys on the shelf, he was talking on the phone. That means though he was physically keeping the keys with his hand, his mind was occupied in the conversation on the phone. Due to this, he did not register the action of placing the keys on the shelf. So it's wrong to say that Rohit has forgotten where he kept the keys 10 minutes before. How can you forget something which you have not registered in the first place?

It is just like searching the whole almirah, taking out everything from it, in an attempt to find a watch you never kept in that almirah. Can you find it? No. It's not possible. So this cannot be called a case of forgetfulness, but a situation of *absentmindedness*.

In order to have stronger memories, we need to involve all our five senses, i.e. *hearing, smell, taste, touch, and sight* as any input to the brain only goes through these five senses. Also, if at that time a strong **association** of the input can be made with some other information already present in our memory. We will discuss the association process in detail in the next chapter, 'Train your memory'.

2. RETENTION: The process of storing the received information for longer duration is called retention. Once the input is done, it should be followed by a system of proper storage so as to retrieve it as and when required. For example, if we go for shopping and buy some books, medicines, clothes, shoes, bread, vegetables etc. and keep them haphazardly all over the house, it would be difficult to find them after a week.

Contrary to this, if these things are stored in their respective places, i.e. books on the bookshelf, medicines in the medicine box, clothes in the wardrobe, shoes in the shoe rack, bread and vegetables in the refrigerator, then each of these things would be easily accessible on time.

LEAKING BRAIN. HELP!

Sara needs to memorize vocabulary words for her SAT exams. She has to memorize nearly 1000 words. She keeps a target of memorizing 40 words per day. She successfully achieves her target on the first day as well as on the second, but as she starts memorizing on the third day, she feels as if she is forgetting the words memorized in the first two days. As the days pass, she finds herself memorizing new words daily but the problem is that she cannot retain the words for long. The more she memorizes, the more she starts getting confused about the earlier memorized words.

Like in the case of Sara, most students find it difficult to retain memorized information till the time of the examination. What good is spending time and effort on memorizing if one cannot retain it till the time it is required.

It's just like a pitcher with a hole which is never going to be filled with water because of constant and continuous leakage.

To avoid this leakage and utilize the unlimited capacity of brain to store information, data needs to be processed and stored systematically.

Strong associations with prior knowledge, clear, vivid, imagery followed by a periodic revision plan are the key steps for retaining any information for longer duration.

3. **RECOLLECTION:** The ability to recollect and use stored information when required is called recollection. Indeed, every action or words we speak are the result of recollection or retrieval of our memories. This process will also yield better results only if the registration and storage of data has been done in an organized and systematic manner. The state of mind at the time of recollection is also a key factor in the process of retrieval.

THE STORY OF EVERY MOTHER

Sheelu is very upset. In spite of working hard with her son, Aditya didn't perform well in his Science exam. She had helped him revise all the question–answers, a night before, was very much sure of him doing well in the exam, but she was astonished when he told her that he had forgotten the answers while writing the exam, though after coming back home he was able to tell the right answers. She couldn't understand why this always happened with him.

As a parent or a student, almost all of us have faced such a situation of helplessness. If we carefully analyze the situation, the problem is not of forgetting, but is of not being able to recollect at the right time, i.e. while taking the exam. Had it been the problem of forgetfulness, how could he recall after the exam? That proves that the answer was there in his memory but he could not recall it at the time of exam when it was most required. Now why did that happen? Because his state of mind at home and the state of mind while giving the exam were not same.

So memory is not just a function of the brain, it is very well guided by the faculty of the MIND, *the creator of thoughts.* By conscious efforts, we can have a better control over our state of mind, thereby resulting in better recollection.

This shows us that all the three stages of memory are equally important. Inefficiency in any of the stages may lead to poor results/memory.

TYPES OF MEMORY

A. ON THE BASIS OF RETENTION PERIOD:

Based on the retention time, Richard Atkinson and Richard Shiffrin developed a multi-store model of memory in 1968, where they categorized memory in 3 types:

1. SENSORY MEMORY
2. SHORT–TERM MEMORY
3. LONG–TERM MEMORY

1. Sensory memory: It is a fleeting type of memory, which works as long as your senses are experiencing a thing. For example: you are looking out of your window watching vehicles passing by, birds flying in the sky, etc. The moment you turn to start doing some work, you will not be able to remember anything unless you have filed any particular information into your short term memory. Whether it is the feel of an object, the smell or sensation of anything, it is all there in the sensory memory for a very brief period while your sense is active.

2. Short-term memory (STM): It holds a small amount of information, typically around seven items or even less for a short period of time, from 10 to 15 seconds, or sometimes up to few minutes. You could probably remember the names of seven people, but once there were more names you would start to forget. We often use this as a tool to remember phone numbers for just long enough to dial them or to remember the direction to an unfamiliar destination. STM helps you recall for as long as you keep thinking about it actively.

Short-term memory is transient and easily interrupted. Therefore, concentration is an important ingredient for keeping things in mind.

> *For example*, you look up a phone number from your address book, and just as you are about to dial the number, you hear someone coming in through the front door. It is likely that you will have to look up the number again. This is because your active memory has been interrupted and you have momentarily lost concentration.

3. Long-term memory (LTM): It lasts from months to years. The data from short-term memory can be transferred to long-term memory by continuous usage and repetition. For example, frequently called phone numbers are remembered because you have used or repeated that number many times. LTM is like a huge hard disk of a giant computer where unlimited information can be stored for a lifetime.

Certain incidents in our life are naturally remembered for a long time. Such events can be negative or positive. *For example,* if we have participated in a school or college competition and won, this memory will almost remain forever. Similarly, if we had a life threatening accident and hardly managed to survive, this event is also almost impossible to forget.

MULTI-STORE MODEL

B. ON THE BASIS OF WAY OF INPUT OF INFORMATION:

1. **Auditory:** When we remember lectures, dialogues or stories we have **heard**, it becomes an auditory memory.
2. **Visual:** When we remember events which we have **seen**, it becomes a visual memory.
3. **Kinesthetic:** The information which is stored in the nerves and muscles and has a movement attached to it is known as kinesthetic memory. While driving a car we change the gears and apply breaks without looking down due to kinesthetic memory. The same is true for eating, walking, dancing, swimming, playing piano, etc.

C. ON THE BASIS OF TYPE OF INFORMATION:

As a child, I was very fond of watching movies. I remember in one of the movies the actor met with an accident and was taken to hospital with serious head injuries. After getting treatment when the actor regained consciousness, the doctor asked him his name and how it all had happened. He answered that he could not recall anything, not even his name, profession, family, nothing. He happened to lose his memory. But the next day, in the movie, he was reading a newspaper. I wondered when he had lost his memory, how could he remember the language he was speaking and how it was possible for him to read a newspaper?

Later when I studied about the human brain, I learnt that our brain have separate parts to deal with information that comes from different senses or different periods or have different levels of importance. A business appointment, the way to a friend's house, or your mother's birthday will all be stored in different parts of the memory.

Based on the kind of information, memory can be categorized as:

1. **Semantic memory**: This is concerned with the storage of factual knowledge like Canberra is the capital of Australia or like paper is made from wood, etc.
2. **Episodic memory**: This is a personal memory for episodes and events; like where I was last night, our last summer vacations, my graduation day at college, etc.
3. **Procedural memory**: This is concerned with learned actions and skills, like swimming, dining, stopping automatically on seeing red traffic light etc.

After learning this, I got to understand that mostly in accidents, *episodic memory is lost, i.e. their personal memory is lost.* That's why they are able to remember all other things, forgetting the people and events related to their personal life.

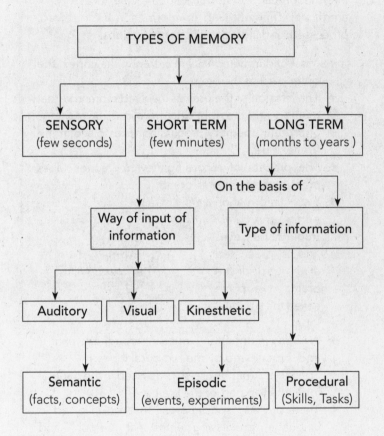

THE BRAIN AND MEMORY

Information can be verbal, visual, tactile, olfactory, or emotional. Different kind of information are received, processed, and stored in different locations:

- ❖ Most of our memories are stored in the cortex (the outer part) of the brain.
- ❖ The left side of the brain is involved more in verbal memory and the right side more in visual memory.
- ❖ Short-term memory processing takes place in the frontal lobe.
- ❖ The process of recording new memories takes place in the temporal lobes.
- ❖ Visual information enters the brain through our eyes and is processed at the back of the brain, in a place called the occipital lobe.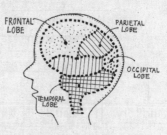
- ❖ Auditory information comes in through the ears and is processed by the temporal lobes.
- ❖ Spatial information is also processed in the parietal lobe, the top part of the brain.
- ❖ There are also special areas that are involved in language, processing emotional memory, and forming habits.

In the next chapter, we will learn how information should be fed into the brain so that we can harness its maximum potential. It's just like learning to arrange various things in the almirah so as to utilize the available space in the best possible manner.

2

ATTENTION—A KEY TO MEMORY

Do you remember the day you bought your first car?
Or met your life partner for the first time?
Or won a medal in school?

Well, I am sure you remember that special day in complete detail. Isn't it surprising that without any knowledge of memory techniques, you are able to remember an event that happened years ago whereas if I ask you about the clothes you wore last Monday, your mind will go blank? Well, there are many situational and natural factors that affect our efficiency of remembering things.

Memory has two principal components to it: **Recording and Recalling**. When new information is safely 'embedded' in the brain, we say it has been *'recorded'*. The recorded information needs to be *'recalled'* to say that we have 'memorized' that information. Stored information that cannot be recalled is like things thrown into a bottomless pit—it is there, but one doesn't know where.

Some natural factors important for converting any information into a memory may be summarized as:

- ✤ Attention
- ✤ Interest
- ✤ Emotions

ATTENTION

Scientists have discovered that in order for the brain to record new information, one of the primary ingredients required is *'Attention'*. Attention is my ability to focus on my chosen task so that the brain processes only that task and 'ignores' the rest of the stimuli.

Attention is like a spotlight—we prevent distraction in our attention through focusing. *For example,* if we are in a room that is noisy, we find it hard to make sense of what a person is saying to us. However, when we focus and become selective in our perception, we find that it becomes easier to catch the voice of the person who is talking to us. This requires focalizing on one sound and ignoring all other sounds as useless.

> **BRAIN FACT**
>
> Any new information that we 'learn' is recorded inside the brain in the form of 'connections' between different neurons called 'neural circuits' and to form a neural circuit, attention is indispensable.

William James, the father of Psychology, said, *'It (attention) is the taking possession by the mind, in clear and vivid form, of one out of what seem several simultaneously possible objects of trains of thoughts.'*

It has been observed in a series of experiments that by merely repeating a task without paying attention to it does not create any new neural circuits inside the brain, i.e., **mere repetition for the** sake of repetition will not get any benefits to you. Studies by memory researchers also show that for **long-term memories to form, close attention has to be paid to information.**

Attention works like a gate, to open and let more neural information in. Without attention, information that our senses take in—what we see and hear, feel, smell, and taste—literally does not register in the mind. It may not be stored even briefly in the memory. Our faculty of attention affects us in countless ways. Our very perception of reality is tied closely to where we focus our attention. Only what we pay attention to seems real to us, whereas whatever we ignore—no matter how important it may be—seems to fade into insignificance.

So we must always pay attention to relevant things so that these stay in our memory for a long time.

INTEREST

When you want to learn and remember something for a longer time, your interest in that particular information plays an equally important role in shaping what you pay attention to.

Rahul is all set to go out to play with his friends when his mom tells him that some friends of his father are coming for dinner. She then tells him a list of things she wants from the market. Rahul listens to it half-heartedly and just as he reaches the shop, he is not able to recall even half of the things he was told to get.

Well, the reason for this is that Rahul was not interested in the list of things his mother was telling him. That is why it did not register strongly in his memory.

This is what happens with most of us in our day-to-day life.

Students don't remember everything they were taught in the lectures they attended in a day. Husbands don't remember what their wives said and kids don't remember even half of the instruction their parents and teachers give them. This is all because of a lack of interest.

On the other hand, **you can easily hold on your attention to things you are interested in.** *For example:* when was the last time you were distracted by thoughts of your homework or forthcoming exams while watching your favourite movie/game/TV serial? Most of you will say *never*. The reason why you were able to concentrate and pay full attention to 3 hours of your favourite movie is because you were interested in watching the movie; hence your attention was uncompromised. Similarly, when you pick a book or attend a class or a lecture, check yourself whether you are interested in it or not. If you think it is boring, you won't be able to focus or pay attention to it. Even while you are being introduced to someone and if you don't pay attention to his name, you won't be able to recall it 5 minutes later, even if it is a simple name. So attention is very important—whether information to be memorized is simple or difficult.

If we are interested in something, we can pay attention to it even if there is so much going around. Nowadays we see people chatting on their smartphones all the time on apps like WhatsApp, Hike etc. While doing so, their complete attention is on that chat. It does not matter if they are in a busy market or travelling in a metro or a local train. Nothing distracts them from their communication with their friend.

Information that interests us is automatically stored as short- or long-term memory, depending on the level of our interest and emotions attached to the information or event. A seven-year-old child can tell you the models of 10 different cars parked in a parking lot but ask him about the spellings he learnt that day in school and he will not remember it. The thought of the cars invoke emotions of pleasure and joy whereas spellings are boring for him. In our daily life we come across people with interest in different things. Some people remember stories of all the novels they read in the last two years or some may remember names of movies of a popular film star. But ask them about the latest Nobel Prize winner and they will not be able to answer because their interest lies elsewhere. But for somebody who is interested in knowing current affairs, it can be just the opposite.

There is one very important thing about **interest**: it **can be generated**. If a person is preparing for the IAS exam, he should develop interest in political and current affairs by reminding himself the benefits of knowing and learning this kind of information for his exams. Interest can be cultivated by reading the newspaper or watching news on TV for it. This will help him in storing the information which can be useful at the time of his exam. Furthermore, the memory techniques discussed in this book offer very unique ways of making any information very interesting through the use of creative visualization and imagination.

EMOTIONS

Emotions play a very important role in maintaining interest in any task. For example, let's say you are a cricket fan and love watching cricket matches. Won't you agree with me that you watch that match with more interest when India is playing against any other country as compared to any two other countries playing a match?

This is because you are emotionally attached to your country India and thus with the Indian cricket team. Similarly, if you are Sachin Tendulkar's fan, you will watch his innings with greater interest as compared to when other players are batting. So emotions play an important role in maintaining our interest in a particular task, event, or situation. In the example given earlier in this chapter, Rahul will be able to memorize the list of things better if his own friends were visiting instead of his father's.

As discussed earlier, you are able to remember some significant days in your life like when you bought your first vehicle, or won a medal in school, or picked a fight with a neighbour, or had some accident in your life, etc. The reason is that some of **your emotions are also attached with these events,** whether positive or negative. In fact emotions act as a *glue* for memory.

For example, you may not remember anything special about getting off your bed the previous morning but if, let's say, 15 days back you stepped on a squeaky toy while getting down from bed, you will not just clearly remember the incident but also the way you were startled by it.

Movies are a big example to clearly explain the impact of emotions in our memory. We remember the story of a few movies we watched years ago because there are so many emotions attached to every scene. We connect ourselves to the characters and feel their emotions of joy or pain so deeply that it gets etched in our memory. All this makes us realize the importance of emotions in memorizing any information.

While remembering emotional (positive or negative) events, we don't just recall whatever happened but also how we felt. **Some memories can be triggered by something we heard, saw, or even smelt at that time.** For example, you visit any famous restaurant and have a good experience there. So the next time you think about that place, you will also remember the aroma of the dish that you liked.

Various researchers and our own experiences suggest that the mood of a person affects what we notice and remember. That is why when we are depressed or sad, we tend to remember all negative events whereas one good memory leads to another. When you go to a wedding, you will find many people discussing things that happened at their own wedding. This is due to their emotional state of celebration.

Our emotional state of mind has a direct impact on our attention. When we are feeling depressed or very excited about something, our mind is occupied with various thoughts. In such a case, our attention drifts off very easily into the thoughts that are occupying our mind.

Without paying attention, as already discussed in detail above, the information won't 'register' inside your brain. *Attention is like a Mental Muscle.* It can be trained to become stronger and sharper. But you should *want* to work on it.

HOW TO IMPROVE ATTENTION

Attention can be improved through **meditation**. Meditation is a form of '**Attention Training**'. It has been proven by scientists that meditation helps in improving attention. It requires practice though. Meditation, by actively engaging your mind on things that are relevant and empowering to you, helps improve concentration by keeping away any *extraneous* thoughts that have the capability to distract you.

Few minutes of daily meditation, in as little as 8 weeks, has been shown to improve people's attention capabilities. You can refer to *Chapter 16, 'How to Improve Concentration'* to understand the technique and importance of meditation in detail.

So if you want to utilize all the techniques listed in this book in order to improve your memory, remember your **AIM—Attention, Interest, and Meditation**. Without AIM, your memory won't improve, however much time you may spend in front of your books.

What we pay attention to, and how we pay attention, determines the content and quality of life.

3

TRAIN YOUR MEMORY

Patient: 'Doctor, I have a serious memory problem. I can't remember anything!'

Doctor: 'So, since when did you have this problem?'

Patient: 'What problem?'

The doctor is shocked!

CAN I HAVE A GOOD MEMORY?

Being a memory trainer, I meet hundreds of people from different professions and lifestyles who are constantly complaining about memory problems. Some people complain that they have a very bad memory and are not able to remember anything while others say that they face problems recalling phone numbers but are good at recalling names and faces. And then there are those who remember phone numbers, but cannot remember the names of the people they wish to call. Some people are fast at memorizing things but cannot retain it for long whereas there are a few others who though take a long time to memorize but can retain that information for a long time. They often ask me to give them some tips on how they can improve their poor memory.

Let me first tell you that **there is no such thing as a poor memory**. This may come as a shock to those of you who have used your supposedly 'poor' memory as an excuse for years. But, I repeat, there is no such thing as a poor memory. There is only **trained or untrained memory**. Trained memory means that we can learn to remember things in a simple and definite way just as we have learnt to speak, walk, and eat. With the use of some smart memory techniques, we can remember much more information for any given length of time, and all this in a very systematic way. The good news is that by training our memory, **we all can have a very good, quick, and retentive memory** for almost anything.

WHAT YOUR UNTRAINED MEMORY CAN DO

Be ready for a small test of your present memory. Read the following list of words:

- ❖ *Ant*
- ❖ *Mobile*
- ❖ *Elephant*
- ❖ *Paintbrush*

- *Poster*
- *Tree*
- *Spiderman*
- *Rainbow*
- *Mug*
- *Biscuits*
- *Lake*
- *Dragon*
- *Cloud*
- *Umbrella*
- *Shoe*

Now, if I ask you to memorize the above list of 15 words in the same sequence, how much time do you think you will take?

When I ask the same question during my seminars, I get responses varying from '15 minutes to 2 hours'. Some people even say, 'We would never be able to memorize it'.

You can take a self-test. Take a stopwatch and try to remember the above list in 3 minutes and after 3 minutes, check how many words you are able to recall in the same sequence correctly. Most of the people are able to recollect the first 4–5 words or last 2–3 words, getting confused in the middle.

Now learn to memorize the above list in less than 2 minutes.

WHAT YOUR TRAINED MEMORY CAN DO

As we have already learnt in the last chapter, registration of information is the first step in the process of memorizing. By adding meaning and structure to the information we take in, we can improve our recall.

Let's say you know only one language i.e. English but this book is written in French. No matter how well things are explained or how relevant the matter is to you, you would not be able to understand it. Unless it makes some sense to you, you won't be able to take it in. In the same way information or data should be fed in a language which the brain can understand.

In computers too we input data through the keyboard, but it is processed through different softwares and is stored in binary language.

Similarly, the brain also takes input through the five senses—hearing, sight, touch, smell, and taste. Since we don't know what processing is required and in which language it should be stored in, we try to register it as it is and that is why registration of information is not done properly.

WHAT IS THAT PROCESSING?

Let's understand it by reading the following passage. While reading, try to visualize it clearly in your mind.

An **ant** is holding a **mobile**. With the mobile, it makes a call to an **elephant**. The elephant is holding a **paintbrush**. With the brush, he is painting a **poster**. This poster is pasted on a **tree**. On top of the tree is a **Spiderman** from whose hands a **rainbow** is coming out instead of web. Rainbow is going into a **mug**, from which a lot of **biscuits** are coming out and falling into a **lake**. In the lake there is a **dragon**, from whose mouth **clouds** are coming out. On the cloud there is an **umbrella** on which a **shoe** is placed.

Now close your eyes and try to repeat it mentally…

Now, without looking back at the story, try to answer the following questions:

1. What was the ant holding?_____
2. Whom is it calling?_____
3. What is the elephant holding? _____
4. What is the elephant painting with the paintbrush? _____
5. The poster is pasted on what? _____
6. What is there on the tree? _____
7. What is coming out of his hands? _____
8. The rainbow is falling into what?_____
9. What is coming out of the mug?_____
10. Where are the biscuits falling? _____
11. What is in the lake?_____
12. What is coming out of the dragon's mouth?_____
13. What is coming out from the cloud?_____
14. What is there on the top of the umbrella? _____

Are you able to answer every question correctly? Awesome! Isn't it?

And the most amazing part is, if you try to recall the words written in bold, you can do it in the same sequence, without actually rote memorizing them!

You must be amazed that what you were unable to do in 10 minutes, you could now could do in just 2 minutes.

How and why you were able to do that?

Irrespective of our academic background, we all have a scientific brain, which is curious to know the *'WHY and HOW'* of everything. Knowing something is different and knowledge of *'how this is useful in my life?'* increases the chances of using it practically.

Let's try to understand the basic principles or laws of memory that will enable you to memorize this list or any such kind of list or sequence.

The three basic laws can be summarized in a single word: **AIR**

LAWS OF MEMORY

As mentioned above, the basic laws or 'principles of memory' can be summarized in a small word i.e., AIR.

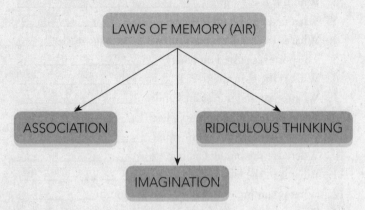

A: ASSOCIATION
Associate the new information with the old information already stored in the mind.

I: IMAGINATION
Imagine that association in the mind and make a clear mental picture of what you want to remember.

R: RIDICULOUS THINKING
Visualize the association in a funny way.

1. LAW OF ASSOCIATION

According to this law, any information can get registered in our brain only if it can be associated or linked with any of the prior information already present in our memory. In fact, all learning till date can be attributed to this law of association. Most of the things you remember have been associated subconsciously with something else that you already knew.

For example, we all know what a line is. If we put four lines of equal length together, end to end, to form a closed figure, we make a square. If we put six squares together, the result will be a cube. Quite simple, but nobody can understand the meaning of a cube without knowing what a line or a square is.

What is true in Geometry is true in every phase of life. **We learn and remember a thing that is new to us only by connecting it with something that we already know.** There is no other way of acquiring knowledge and we have been doing this throughout our life. We may not always be aware of this process, but we make associations regularly.

Association means linking what you want to remember with something you already know.

In fact, our brain always stores information in the form of associations or connections. Whenever a stimulus comes from outside, it recalls the connection. *For example*, you are thinking about your school friend. Immediately, you will be reminded of many things associated with your friend like the time you spent together, your school, classroom, class teacher, etc. Similarly, when we think about a bird, along with it we are reminded of nest, eggs, sky, and tree.

Can you think of any one thing to which no other information is related? According to scientists this is impossible since our brain can memorize information only in pairs. For example, if someone asks you to memorize a random date like 18th February, 1985, it is illogical for us to memorize it. When this date gets associated with the name of any person or event, we can then memorize it. This is because our brain memorizes only connections and for connecting, we need two elements of information.

Given below are some examples from a simple word association game that children often play for amusement:

Call word	Response
Chair	Table
Son	Father
Examination	Study
Dark	Light
Black	White
Rain	Water

Thus we find that we instantly recall something after having read a particular word, although we may not have thought about that thing for months. You can easily find an association or relation between the given word and the respective answer.

➢ Now try it for yourself. Write down what comes to your mind immediately after reading the following words:

❖ *Sachin Tendulkar* _____
❖ *Books* _____
❖ *Pen* _____
❖ *Window* _____
❖ *Cup* _____
❖ *Party* _____

Association simply means that when one word or idea is presented, another word or idea, with which the first word is connected, is recalled.

Try to recall the list of 15 words you memorized in the beginning of this chapter, starting from Ant, and write all of them in the space given below:

_____
_____
_____
_____
_____
_____

_____

_____

_____

_____

_____

_____

_____

_____

I am sure you have successfully recalled nearly all of them in the same sequence.

Now let's play a little trick!

Try to recall and write what was after elephant: _____

Now check if you can correctly tell what was before elephant:

_____

Write what is after dragon:_____

Once you have written your answers, refer to the list and check. I am sure all your answers are correct.

Whether I ask you something from the middle of the list or from the end, you are able to answer it so fast because when I ask elephant, it is linked to paintbrush in the forward order and is associated with mobile in the reverse order. The moment I give you one information, the other one connected to it is recalled automatically without any effort of going into the sequence of the whole list.

ASSOCIATIONS ARE LIKE PEARLS IN A NECKLACE

If I have a fist full of pearls and I put them on a table, chances are that they will get scattered here and there. Some of them might roll down the edge of the table and disappear. Some might remain on the table, constantly changing their position. After five minutes, it would be difficult for me to collect all of them in my hand. But if I put all these pearls in a string and tie a knot and place it on the table, all the pearls will remain in the same place, making it easy for me to pick them up, wear them, use them, and place them back in my drawer without losing any of the pearls.

Associating information with each other is quite similar to putting pearls in a string. Initially, when I asked you to memorize the list, most of you might have been able to recall the first 2–3 words or the last few ones, but not the ones in the middle. That's because all words were scattered in the memory like pearls on a table. But through association, we connected the first word with the second, then second with third and so on, so the information is secured in your memory. That is why even now you can recall any word from the list in the correct sequence. *That is the beauty of association.*

We have been using this association technique consciously in some ways earlier also. For example, most of us must have used the famous phrase—*'My Very Educated Mother Just Served Us Noodles'* to memorize the sequence of eight planets in our solar system through the initials of the words *(i.e. Mercury Venus Earth Mars Jupiter Saturn Uranus Neptune)*.

Many a times we are not able to make an association of all the information required to remember. In this book you are going to learn how to associate anything you want to remember, and the wonderful part about the whole thing is that after using this system consciously for a while, you will automatically start using it as a natural process.

2. LAW OF IMAGINATION

Law of Association does not work in isolation. It works well with the Law of Imagination or Visualization.

Imagining a thing or an event once is equivalent to hearing about it twenty times. **Our human brain remembers pictures better.** Whatever we see, we tend to retain that information for a much longer period of time as compared to what we hear. This is because the nerves connecting the eyes to the brain are twenty times more powerful than the nerves that connect the ears to the brain. Has it happened that sometimes we meet someone whose face seems very familiar but we are unable to recall his/her name?

Now think again...

Has it ever happened that you remember a person's name but do not remember his face when you meet him?

No, right? This is because a **face is something we see and a name is something we hear**. Seeing something forms a permanent memory in our brain. In fact, try to recall any memory from the past—your graduation day at college or your first interview or your first anniversary. As you are reading this, images of those memories must have started forming in your mind because brain stores memories in the form of pictures.

From the list of 15 words, when I asked you what was after 'elephant', were you not able to give me the right answer without following the complete sequence? Why? Because while recollecting you were not referring to the list. Rather when I said elephant, immediately an image *(which you created while reading and visualizing that passage)* flashed into your mind and you gave the answer just by referring to that image. That is why recollection was so fast and spontaneous.

This is the power of **Imagination**. Instead of visualizing, if you had just mugged up that list, you definitely would have had to go in the sequence, putting a lot of stress on your mind just to recollect the next word.

That means if I can consciously convert any information into an image, I can keep it in my memory for a much longer period of time. *Just like you have memorized a list of simple 15 words*, we can remember anything, even abstract words, foreign language or points of speech/ lectures, etc. by using the power of **imagination** along with association.

The key to *an impressive* imagination is the third law, i.e. *Law of Ridiculous Thinking*.

3. LAW OF RIDICULOUS THINKING

According to this law, whatever is odd, silly, funny, outstanding, strange, weird, unusual, or ridiculous, our brain tends to register it fast and is able to retain that information for a longer period of time. Our mind is attracted to unusual and outstanding things, events, or people.

While reading the story mentioned earlier, you visualized weird things.

- ❖ Have you ever seen an ant talking on a mobile?
- ❖ Have ever seen an elephant painting on a poster?
- ❖ Can you believe an umbrella can be on top of a cloud?

All these things were strange and ridiculous and that is the reason you were able to memorize them so fast.

So, if you can purposefully and deliberately make your associations funny, then you can retain it for a longer period. In a nutshell, we learn that the principle of AIR—**A**ssociation, **I**magination, and **R**idiculous thinking—can help us to register any information with easy, fast, and accurate recollection.

KEY TO REGISTER ANY INFORMATION

Associate two or more pieces of information while imagining them, using ridiculous thinking.

We will explore the principle of AIR in detail in the following chapters of this book, which will enable us to memorize a lot many things from our day-to-day life.

PART B.

MEMORY TECHNIQUES AND
THEIR APPLICATIONS

4

MAKING STRONG ASSOCIATIONS

Now that you have learnt the laws of memory, it's time to take up a challenge and see how you can apply these laws. How about you go to your best friend and tell him that your memory has become very strong and that **you can memorize a list of 10 objects** in the same sequence, **without writing it anywhere,** and that too in just a few seconds? But before taking on the challenge, let's practice it once.

Just imagine me as your friend who gives you a list of 10 words to memorize.

Now let's see how you can memorize it using the *principle of AIR*, i.e. *a*ssociating one word with the next while *i*magining it in a *r*idiculous (funny) way.

The list is:

> *BOOK*
> *BLACK RABBIT*
> *SWIMMING POOL*
> *MANGOES*
> *YELLOW BIRD*
> *RED HAT*
> *BUTTERFLY*
> *WHITE HORSE*
> *SNOW WHITE*
> *LAPTOP*

1. Let's start by associating the *first* word **'Book'** with the *second* word **'Black Rabbit'**. Visualize that you are holding a book and it is very thick. Try to feel its weight. It's so heavy that you can barely manage to hold it. As you open the book, you see a picture of a black rabbit. Suddenly the rabbit starts growing in size. It becomes real and alive  and comes out of the book. Just as you try to touch it to feel it's soft and shinning skin, it jumps out of your hand, makes a face, and challenges you by saying 'Catch me if you can!'

2. Now associate Black Rabbit with the next word—**'Swimming Pool'**. Visualize yourself following the black rabbit running towards a swimming pool. He jumps into it, splashing water all around, making you wet. People in the pool are taken aback and you can hear their screams.

3. Swimming Pool and **Mangoes**—Visualize that the swimming pool is full of mangoes and everyone is playing with mangoes like one plays with balls.

4. Mangoes and **Yellow Bird**—Suddenly all the mangoes burst open and a yellow bird appears from each mango. Visualize that they are all flying in the sky. The sky seems full of yellow birds.

5. Yellow Bird and **Red Hat**—Visualize one of the yellow birds wearing a big red hat like a British lady. She is looking very pretty in it.

6. Red Hat and **Butterfly**—Visualize the bird holding the red hat in her hand and waving it like a princess, making graceful gestures towards people. Just as she raises her hat, a butterfly flies from beneath. Now see the butterfly flying down towards you.

7. Butterfly and **White Horse**—Visualize the butterfly coming near you. As it comes closer, it gets transformed into a white horse. You are very glad to see him as you touch his soft mane.

8. White Horse and **Snow White**—Visualize that just as you were about to sit on the white horse, Snow White came running from behind, knocked you down, sat on the horse, and rode him away.

9. Snow White and **Laptop**—Visualize Snow White waving her hand in the air and by magic, a laptop appears. She herself disappears in the dust, throwing the laptop towards

you. You manage to catch it carefully and place it on the ground.

Now try to visualize it again in your mind in detail and see if you can recall all 10 words. I am sure if you have visualized all the associations well, you would have been able to recall all 10 words.

Let's make this task a little more challenging. I am going to give you **5 more words** to be added to the list Read each word slowly and while reading, visualize the first word and link it with the last word in the above list i.e. laptop. Then read the next word and associate it with the previous word, while visualizing it in a funny way, exactly as we did in the above list. Do it till all 5 words are associated. The words are:

SPIDERMAN

TUNNEL

TARZAN

STONES

PAINTING BRUSH

HINT: Start by associating Spiderman with the last word Laptop in a funny way. After doing this exercise, try to recall all 15 words in a sequence while visualizing the associations in your mind. You can also try recalling in reverse order.

Now you have learnt how to use the principle of AIR practically to memorize a list of 15 words in a sequence. Using the same technique, **we can succeed in remembering a sequence of even a hundred words!**

Thus we can go on associating any two items in a fantastic, imaginary way. The objects to be remembered are linked to one another, forming a chain, and that is why this method is called the **CHAIN METHOD.** In this method, the first object is linked to the second, the second to the third and so on. This is also called the **STORY METHOD** as we sometimes weave a story about the things to remember.

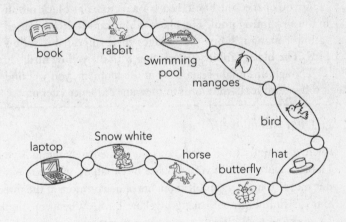

This chain method or story method is the most commonly used memory technique and is very easy to understand and use. This method can be useful for memorizing *shopping lists, points of presentations, answers* and many other important things from our day-to-day life. We will elaborate on this more in the next chapter.

Points to remember:

At any point of the association, always work with just two words at a time. If you remember, while memorizing those 15 words, I first associated **book** with a **black rabbit**. Once I did this, I didn't think of the word 'book' any more. I proceeded to the next pair of words, i.e. **black rabbit** and **swimming pool**. Again, once I did this, I stopped thinking about the rabbit and simply associated my next pair of words, i.e. **swimming pool** and **mangoes**. At any given point, I was only working with associating two words at a time.

When you are a beginner in memory techniques, it's very natural to create a story connecting all the words. *For example,* let's say you imagined your associations like this:

As you opened the **book**, you saw a picture of a **black rabbit** in the **swimming pool**. The **black rabbit** came out and started eating a **mango**. From the **mango**, there appeared a **yellow bird**. **The black rabbit** starts playing with the **yellow bird**.

Though this might seem okay at the moment, you will find it difficult to recall the words in the same sequence later on.

See what will happen?

When you think of the word 'book', it immediately reminds you of a black rabbit. When you visualize black rabbit, what comes to your mind? It may trigger off thoughts of one or more of the three things (swimming pool, mango, yellow bird). When you think of swimming pool, does it remind you of the next word mango? Chances are that it doesn't.

Now check it for yourself. In my original associations, the word book is **only** linked with the black rabbit. Further on, the black rabbit is linked with a swimming pool which is further linked to mangoes…and so on, resulting in recollection without any confusion.

> **In a Nutshell:** Always link two words at a time when using the chain method. The first word should be linked only to the second, the second only to the third and so on. The first word should not be linked again to the fourth. Likewise, the second should not be linked to any other word except the first and the third.

HOW TO MAKE STRONG ASSOCIATIONS?

Sometimes people say that '**we are not good at imagining things**' or '**cannot make as strong an association between words as you make**'. They claim that they tend to recall better when they remember using my associations or when I make them visualize an association. **I would say it's just the opposite**.

Just think of how well you remember the story of your favourite movie, starring your favourite actor. Sometimes you can recall each scene of the movie as well as its dialogues. Now think about a movie where **YOU** are the actor, director, producer, editor, and dialogue writer. *Can you forget the movie?* It's just not possible.

Similarly, it's not possible for you to forget the visualization you have created yourself.

It is important to know that **you can associate two things in whichever way you want.** There is no set track for making associations. In fact, whenever you try to associate two words, most of the time more than one association will come to your mind. Try to choose the one that seems most illogical and ridiculous, something that does not happen every day. For e.g. if you have to associate two words **'book'** and **'house'**, you can visualize different associations between the two. For instance,

1. A house is made up of books instead of bricks.
2. A house is full of books.
3. As you open the book, a big house came out of it as a gift for you.
4. A big book is the foundation of a house built on it.
5. A book full of pictures of different types of houses.

Try to think of many other such associations. Write two sample associations below:

_____

_____

_____

_____

KEY POINTS FOR BETTER VISUALIZATION

Usually we are taught to think logically, and here I am telling you to make illogical or ridiculous pictures. I know some of you might face problems in the beginning in making up ridiculous pictures in your mind. Let us help you in this matter by sharing simple rules of AEIOU:

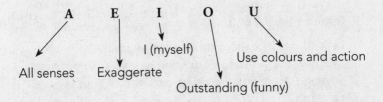

A: All senses
E: Exaggerate (think out of proportion)
I: I (myself)
O: Outstanding
U: Use colours and action

1. **A:** *All senses*—Try to visualize the picture or association with all your senses. Make it as alive as possible. The more the numbers of senses we use, the deeper forms the impression in our brain. Your association should be visualized in the form of clear images, including sound, smell, touch, and taste, if possible. *For example*, if we have to make an association between a bed sheet and roses, there are two ways of doing it. One, you just imagine a bed sheet with roses printed on it or second, you can imagine the bed sheet in more detail—the roses start being real, the room is full of its mesmerizing *smell*, their petals are *soft* to touch, etc. If you go by the second way, you are more likely to remember it for a longer time because when we involve more senses, that information is stored in more parts of our brain, resulting in a deeper impression and a better recall.

MAXIMIZE THE USE OF SENSES

Let's say, you are **listening to a recipe on the radio**. You will try your best to pay attention to it so as to not miss anything. Here you are using only one of your senses, i.e. *ears*.

Now, let's assume you are **watching a cookery show** on television. There you can see the details of preparing the dish like for how much time you have to cook the vegetable to make it equally tender or if you are making a batter then how much consistency should it have etc. Here you are using two of your senses—*eyes and ears*.

Now visualize yourself **attending a live cookery class**. There you can actually feel the texture of the ingredients. You can feel and learn how hard or soft the dough should be, how coarse or fine the puree should be, you can smell the aroma while listening to each instruction and observing each step carefully, and finally you can taste it too.

In your opinion, in which case from the above would the learning be better and faster and you will be able to retain the method for a longer period of time?

Obviously in the third case because you are taking in the information using all five senses.

To sum up, we have to use most of our senses while imagining things for effective memory.

While associating a Book with a Black Rabbit, I asked you to visualize the thickness of the book, feel its weight, and see the black rabbit in action, growing in size. Visualize its colour, its shine of the skin, feel of the skin, and then finally the action of jumping out from the book and challenging you to catch him. So you made use of three of your senses: sight, touch, and hearing. That helps you feel the moment as real, as if you are a part of this event and bringing in three dimensions and movement to an image makes it more real.

2. **E:** *Exaggeration*—Visualize the objects in an exaggerated or out of proportion manner, especially in size or quantity. *For example*, visualizing so many yellow birds in the sky or one elephant-sized yellow bird makes more impact on the brain as compared to a single normal-sized bird.

3. **I:** *Myself*—Imagine that you are given photographs of a party that you attended some time back. Who will you look for in the photographs? Obviously yourself! Most of the time we are interested only in our self, i.e. 'I' or something associated with 'I'. So the picture that you are going to imagine should include you, doing some action. That is why, while imagining the list given above, I asked you to visualize yourself holding a book—**you** are touching the horse's mane, **you** went to sit on the horse, or **you** caught the laptop.

4. **O:** *Outstanding*—Try to visualize an image that is strange, odd, different from normal, outstanding, or silly. Our brain has a tendency to remember peculiar things.

5. **U:** *Use colours and actions in your image*—Would you like to see a black and white TV or a coloured one? Involvement of colours makes the picture unique and interesting. In the same way, action makes images appear more interesting compared to static images, that is why I used action while visualizing the list.

Applying any combination of these five principles when forming your images will help make your mental associations truly outstanding and memorable. At first, you may need to consciously apply one or more of the five principles, but after a little practice, their application will become an automatic and natural process.

Try visualizing an association between the following pairs keeping in mind the principle of **AEIOU.**

1. Banana and Donkey
    _____
    _____
    _____
    _____

2. Ice-cream and Table
    _____
    _____
    _____
    _____

It's not important how long you visualize a picture,

It's more important how clear you visualize it.

CHAPTER AT A GLANCE

❖ We can memorize any information given in the form of a list or a sequence by forming creative associations using the chain method.

❖ In this, one object is associated with the second, second with the third and so on, like rings in a chain.

❖ The items can be linked simply one after the other, like the rings in a chain, or we can weave a story to link all the objects given in the list.

❖ Points to remember for making strong associations:
  ➢ Link only two words at a time.
  ➢ First word should be linked to the second, second to the third and so on.
  ➢ Do not link one word to many different words as it might create confusion.

❖ Use the principle of AEIOU for better visualization:

  A: All senses—Make associations using all senses.
  E: Exaggerate (think out of proportion) the visualization.
  I: I (myself)—Try including yourself while imagining an association.
  O: Outstanding—The image should be outstanding, i.e. different than usual, silly, not normal.
  U: Use colours and action in your imagination.

Using these five principles will enable you to create memorable associations.

5

APPLICATION OF CHAIN METHOD

The **'Chain Method'** is a quick way to connect unrelated items like the ones on a random list or any reading material. The idea is to create effective links between pairs of items in such a way that when you think of one item, the next one immediately comes to mind.

We can create a chain of words in two ways:

1. It can be just pure linking where each word is just associated with the next, or

2. You can weave a story around the items to make the learning more interesting and permanent.

This method has varied applications. It can be used to memorize a shopping list, grocery list, checklist, things-to-do on a particular day, points of speech or presentation, points to be discussed in a meeting, questions–answers, and many more important things.

MEMORIZING A SHOPPING LIST

We all have a habit of making a list of things to buy from a grocery store, but many a times we forget to carry the list along. Or sometimes we forget to carry the tabs or mobile phones in which we have noted down the list in our car or at home. For people with whom this is a common occurrence, the 'Chain Method' is a life saviour using which you can easily memorize all the items in just a few minutes.

Given below is a sample shopping list that includes common items. Your list may vary a little but the method to memorize it will be the same.

Toothbrush

Shampoo

Biscuits

Tomatoes

Reebok sports shoes

Pen

Honey

Mobile recharge

Notebook

Popcorn

Let's try to remember this list using the chain method:

Just imagine yourself standing outside the shop holding a huge **toothbrush** as tall as you. Now imagine that instead of toothpaste you are putting **shampoo** on it.

As soon as you try to put it in your mouth, it starts raining and instead of raindrops, **biscuits** start pouring from the sky.

To cover yourself you run to a nearby tomato field. There you see bright red **tomatoes** as big as a football. As soon as you pick up the biggest tomato on the field, you find glittering blue **Reebok sports shoes** under it.

As you start trying to wear one of them, a magic **pen** emanating a green light pops out from it. You take that pen and start running but suddenly you fall into a big tub. You realize that it is filled with **honey**. Now imagine yourself totally covered with sticky honey.

You feel dirty and take out your mobile phone from your pocket to call for help. As soon as you try dialling the number, you get a message that there is no balance in your phone. You realize that you were supposed to get your **phone recharged**.

With a lot of difficulty, you manage to come out and reach a phone booth. There you find a **notebook** that has big yellow flowers on its cover. You note down your mother's number on it and give it to a lady operating the phone booth. You request her to dial this number.

Upon seeing your condition, she offers you some **popcorn** and calls your mother who comes to take you home.

Now after reading the above paragraph, try recalling the list.

I am sure most of you will be able to do it. In case you are not able to visualize the things properly in your mind and are facing difficulty in recalling it, don't get disheartened. With practice, and by learning other techniques in the coming chapters, I am sure you will be able to improve your visualization and recall.

As I mentioned earlier, each person will have a different list, so you can imagine a chain of events according to your list.

As Many As You Want

You can memorize as long a list as you want; there is no limit to it. You will find no problem doing this, since at one point of time you are making associations between two words only and are visualizing only one image at a time. As we know, the brain has immense potential for remembering images, so it will not get confusing even if you have to memorize a list 50 or 100 words or more. One of our students, made a national record by memorizing 507 words in the same sequence only after listening to them once.

MEMORIZING A LIST OF 'THINGS -TO-DO' TODAY

In our day-to-day life, we play so many roles like that of a parent, a son/daughter, a boss, a subordinate, or a friend. While playing those roles we have so many duties and responsibilities to fulfil that it makes our life hectic. One way that we usually follow to plan our day is to make a to-do-list. Now how to remember that?

You might ask why *you should try to remember it* when you can comfortably write it on a piece of paper and later refer to it throughout the day while doing your chores. Well that's true, but it's not always possible to refer to your to-do list in-between every task. Also, the chances of misplacing that piece of paper or diary are very high. It makes much more sense to note down your to-do list and then spend a few more minutes to memorize it using *AIR*.

For example, let's take a list of tasks that you have to do (in sequence) on a particular Saturday.

> Playing **lawn tennis** at your club in the morning
> Washing the **car**
> Going to the **bank** for depositing a cheque
> Getting a **hair cut**
> Buying **medicines**
> Visiting your **dentist**
> Visiting a **stationery shop** to buy a few things, like a **hand-made sheet, markers, crayons, and stapler**
> Picking up a stitched dress from the **boutique**
> Helping your **son** in completing his school **project**
> Preparing for your presentation **which is due next week**
> Baking a **cake**

The bold words can be taken as the keywords to be remembered which will further remind you of the complete task to be done. For example, just a mention of the car is enough to remind you that it has to be washed.

Now make associations between the tasks using the chain method. Just to help you out, an idea for the visualization is given below.

VISUALIZATION:

Saturday is the only day when you get to meet your friends in the **club**. Visualize that in the club you are playing **lawn tennis** with your friends. After playing, you and your friends start washing your **car** which is completely covered in mud. You get into your shining, freshly washed car and straight away drive into the **bank**. The people in the bank attack you and start giving you a **haircut**. You fight with them and in the process, you get a cut on your neck. You rush to buy **medicines** from a nearby store. There you see that your **dentist** is selling medicines. He starts examining your teeth using **stationary items** as his tools. He covers your body with **hand-made paper**, colours your teeth with **crayons** and red **marker** and after that he **staples** your mouth. To remove all these, you rush to your **boutique** where the tailor helps you in removing that paper and gives you your newly stitched dress. You use that dress for your **son's project**. Your son gets an award for his **presentation**. You celebrate the success by baking a chocolate **cake**.

After you have associated all your things-to-do for the day, all you have to do is complete one task and that will remind you of the next, and so on.

You will learn how to remember this list with time details as well when we learn to remember appointments using the number pegging system in chapter 12 'Peg System'.

MEMORIZING A CHECKLIST

On the second day of my 3-day long Mind and Memory Workshop for students organized in a college, a participant shared his experience of using the chain method in his personal life. I had taught them the chain method on the first day of the workshop. He told me that his apartment was on the sixth floor and most of the time while leaving for college he would feel as if he was forgetting to pick up something. Because of this, he would check again to make sure he had taken everything he needed so that he didn't have to come up again. But by the time he would reach the ground floor, he would find that he had actually forgotten something important at home. Sometimes it was his mobile phone or bike keys or sometimes his important notes. This would lead to a lot of wastage of time and energy.

But after learning the chain technique of memorizing, he learnt to apply it successfully to memorize all the things without missing anything.

Here is the list that he shared with the other participants at the workshop:

- *Wallet*
- *Identity card*
- *Watch*
- *Mobile*
- *Sunglasses*
- *Water bottle*
- *Books*
- *Handkerchief*
- *Keys*

Now let's try to make a chain for the above list.

Just imagine it's your birthday and your mother gives you a brown leather **wallet** as gift. You put some cash in it and try to insert your **I-card.** But the card is too big. So you tie this card to your *watch* with a string and wear the watch. Your watch turns into a **mobile** that starts ringing loudly. It's your sister who calls to wish you and tells you that she has bought big, black *sunglasses* as your birthday gift...

Now complete this chain using your own imagination.

_____

_____

_____

_____

Similarly you can also practice memorizing the following given checklist of things to be taken by a student to a folder-making competition. The list is:

- *Handmade paper*
- *Broken CD pieces*
- *Quilling strips*
- *Glue*
- *Silver string*
- *Quilling tool*
- *Scissors*
- *Sketch pens*
- *Yellow highlighter*
- *Stapler*
- *Ruler*
- *Pencil box containing pencil, rubber, and sharpener*

Write your visualization:

_____

_____

_____

_____

Students can use this wonderful technique to memorize key points of their answers for faster recollection during exams. For more details and examples, you can check the students section where a combination of two or more techniques has been used to memorize long answers, vocabulary words, formulae, periodic table, scientific terms, and other relevant information.

The chain method is probably the most basic memory technique, and is very easy to understand and use. However, its reliability depends on the user remembering the sequence of images or events in a story. It is obvious that if an image is missing from the sequence, or if an element is forgotten, some or all following images may be lost as well. If the visualization is clear and vivid, chances are that a person will definitely recall everything memorized through this method with cent percent accuracy.

CHAPTER AT A GLANCE

❖ The *Chain Method* is a quick way to connect unrelated items on any given list.
❖ It is the most basic memory technique which is very easy to use and understand.
❖ It includes creating effective links between pairs of items to enable easy recall.
❖ We can create a chain of words in two ways:
  ➤ By linking each word with the next.
  ➤ By weaving a story around the items to make the learning more interesting and permanent.
❖ This method can be used to memorize things like:
  ➤ Shopping list
  ➤ To-do list
  ➤ Checklist
  ➤ Points of speech or presentation
  ➤ Points to be discussed in a meeting etc.
  ➤ Key points in answers to important questions

6

PERSONAL NICK NAME (PNN) METHOD

A few old couples would get together occasionally to talk about life and have a good time. One day one of the men, Rohit, started talking about this fantastic restaurant he had been to the other night with his wife: 'Really?', one of the men asked, 'what's it called?'

After thinking for a few seconds, Rohit said, 'What are those good smelling flowers called again?'

'Do you mean a rose? the first man questioned.

'Yes that's it,' he exclaimed. Looking over at his wife he said, 'Rose, what's that restaurant we went to the other night?'

Till now we have tried to memorize a list of words that we are familiar with, therefore we could create a mental picture of them the moment we heard them. But what if we need to memorize difficult, unfamiliar words or names of new places or people about whom we don't have any image in our mind? For instance, words like Ukraine, helium, exorbitant, etc. For that we have to learn a new method called the *Personal Nick Name Method.*

PNN (PERSONAL NICK NAME) METHOD

When we hear a difficult or long name of a person, we usually give it a short (nick) name so that it becomes easy to pronounce. In the same way, when we come across any new or difficult word, we should pronounce it slowly, so as to find a familiar word similar to its pronunciation or a related image already stored in our personal memory. We can use that word as a nickname for the new word. This method of giving a nickname to a new word is known as **Personal Nick Name (PNN) method**. It is called 'personal' as nicknames may vary from person to person. Nickname can be one word or a group of words.

NICK NAME IT!

Suppose you need to visualize a country name, like **Poland**. At first, it will be difficult for you to visualize this word in your mind if you have never been there. But through the PNN system, when we pronounce Poland slowly as *PO –L – AND*, some familiar words we can find in it are:

+ 'Pole'or
+ 'Pole on Land' or
+ 'Pole + Ant' or
+ 'Polar Bear' or
+ 'Polo' (mint)

Some other words may come to your mind depending upon your imagination. Different people may think of different nicknames in a word, that's why it is known as the *personal* nick name method, as it not fixed and depends on one's imagination and earlier vocabulary.

Now a word like Poland, which was earlier difficult for you to visualize, is a clear image for you.

This PNN method is useful for memorizing difficult, abstract words, technical terms, scientific terminology, general facts and information, names of people and places, etc. But before learning to memorize these, lets first see some examples to understand how to break up abstract words or names into familiar words and images.

Some examples are:

	Abstract Words	Personal Nick Name	Image (funny)
1.	Honesty	Ho – nest – y	Nest
2.	Diligent	Dell + agent (*Computer Brand*)	*Agent* is selling *Dell* Computer
3.	Vijaywada	Vijay + Wada (Name of Person) (South Indian dish)	*Vijay* is eating *Wada*
4.	Rajendra Prasad	Raja + Prasad	*Raja* is distributing *Prasad*
5.	Ukraine	U (you) + Crane	You are lifting a crane

	Abstract Words	Person-al Nick Name	Image (funny)
6.	Slovakia (country)	Slow + walk (vakia)	A person is *walking* very *slowly*
7.	Helium (element)	Heel + yumm	A man is eating the high *heel* of a sandal and saying 'Yummm…'
8.	Exorbitant	Ex – orbit – ant *(out)*	An *ant* is moving *out* of its *orbit* around the Earth
9.	Cosmic Rays	Cosmet-ics + rays	*Cosmetics* are coming out in the form of *rays*.
10.	Chromite	Crow + mite	A *mighty crow*

It is not always necessary to make PNN according to a similar sound of the given word. Infact, any **other knowledge or related image can serve as a nick name** for that word. Let's take '*Australia*'—when you pronounce it slowly as *Aus – tra – lia*, it sounds like *Os – tri – ch* (Ostrich) or it may sound like *Ash – tray*. But on hearing Australia, if someone is reminded of '*Kangaroo*', then he/she can take **Kangaroo** as the nick name for **Australia**.

Similarly, **'Agra'** reminds me of the famous **'Taj – Mahal'** or the **'Congress'** (political party of India) reminds me of **'Sonia Gandhi'**. So, we can take these as the PNN of the respective words.

Some more such examples:

Words	Related image/ Knowledge	Image to visualize
Switzerland	Switzerland is famous for *watches*	Designer watches
Gujarat	*Dandia* dance is famous in Gujarat	People dancing in dandia dress
Amritsar	*Golden Temple*	Golden temple
Srilanka	*Ravan* (from Ramayana)	Ravan
Beauty	*Aishwarya Rai*	Aishwarya Rai
Africa	*Forests*	Forests

Use of PNN makes it possible to convert any abstract word, phrase, technical term, business jargon, difficult vocabulary word, or foreign language word into a picture. So you can visualize it and can associate the related information with them easily.

HOW TO MEMORIZE COUNTRIES AND CAPITALS

Using association and PNN method, we can memorize confusing and difficult names of various countries and capitals. For example: You are reading about a country called **Bulgaria** and you need to memorize that its capital is *Sofia*. At first it will be difficult for you to visualize these words in your mind. Using the PNN system, when we pronounce Bulgaria slowly as *BUL – GA – RIA*, a familiar word we can find in it is 'Bull' or one can say '*Bull gir gaya*' or '*bull in a grey area*'.

The capital of Bulgaria is **Sofia**; a familiar word in it can be 'Sofa'.

Now make an association between the two. Visualize in your mind that a **<u>Bull</u> is lying on your <u>Sofa</u>.**

A funny image like this would be difficult to forget. When you will be asked about Bulgaria, a bull will come in your mind along with the sofa which will help you to recall the capital Sofia.

The above example shows how visualization with association helps you to learn the things faster.

Some more examples:

		PNN	VISUALIZATION
Country	Barbados	Barbie Doll	A town of *Barbie dolls* is located on a *bridge*.
Capital	Bridgetown	A Town on a Bridge	

		PNN	VISUALIZATION
Country	Australia	Ostrich	An *ostrich* is taking photographs using a *camera*.
Capital	Canberra	Camera	

The capital of Australia is Canberra. This can also be memorized by creating some other PNN of Australia as per your choice, like if **Kangaroo** *(its national animal)* or **Ricky Ponting** *(Australian Cricket player)* come into your mind, when you think about Australia, you can associate them with Camera *(PNN of Canberra)*.

If you take Kangaroo, you can visualize that *'A Kangaroo jumps on you and snatches the camera from your hand'.*

		PNN	VISUALIZATION
Country	Ukraine	You + Crane	*You* are lifting gigantic *Kiwis* with a *crane*.
Capital	Kiev	Kiwi (fruit)	

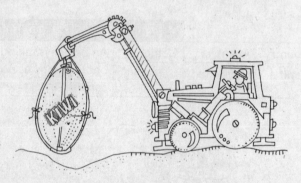

The beauty of the method is that not only are you able to memorize countries with their capitals, you also don't get confused while recalling the name. Mostly when we memorize such facts, we tend to mix up the information. But here the chances of making mistakes are negligible. For example, if I ask you *what do you remember of Barbados?*

An image of a *Barbie Doll* will appear in your mind and if you have visualized it clearly, only a related image of a *town of Barbie on a bridge* will be recalled. No other picture can come to your mind due to the association technique.

Now try to memorize the following sites and their places using the PNN method. Some nick names and their visualization are given for you. For others, make your own PNN and visualize them:

S.NO.	SITE	PLACE
1.	Inamgao	Maharashtra
2.	Yangtze River	China
3.	Jog falls	Karnataka
4.	Alps	Europe
5.	Ural Mountains	Russia
6.	Chirand	Bihar

		PNN	VISUALIZATION
Site	Inamgao	Inam (prize)	*Maharaja* is distributing *inam* to everybody
Place	Maharashtra	Maharaja	
Site	Yangtze River	Young + River (young girl in river)	A young girl is making chai (tea) with river water
Place	China	Chai (tea)	
Site	Jog falls	Jogging	
Place	Karnataka	Kar – natak	
Site	Alps	Apes	
Place	Europe	Rope	

Site	Ural Mountains		
Place	Russia		

Site	Chirand		
Place	Bihar		

MYTH

Many people think that if we memorize things by making pictures of everything and then associating them, our mind will be full of pictures and we might get confused.

BUSTED

Our brain has a limited capacity for words, but an unlimited capacity for images or pictures.

SELF REALIZATION

Since morning, *can you count how many images have you seen till now?*

Do you feel that your brain is full and that you can no longer see more images?

'NO'. In fact, even if you close your eyes, more pictures will come into your mind because our mind thinks in pictures and is continuously thinking of something or the other. Even while asleep, thoughts keep coming in the form of dreams.

So, *do not worry.* Even if you stop making visualizations to remember something, your mind will continue to see pictures. Then why not use it purposefully for your own benefit?

HOW TO MEMORIZE ANSWERS USING *PNN* AND *CHAIN* METHOD

Now let's see how we can use this method to memorize answers.

Q. List out the various processes employed in the separation of components of a mixture.

Ans. The various processes employed in the separation of components of a mixture are as follows:

1. Winnowing
2. Hand-picking
3. Sieving
4. Decantation
5. Filtration
6. Magnetic Separation
7. Loading
8. Churning
9. Evaporation

Hint: Suggested PNN (you can create your own as well)

Winnowing	Window
Hand-picking	Hand
Sieving	Sieve
Decantation	Canteen
Filtration	Filter machine
Magnetic Separation	Magnet
Loading	Load
Churning	Churn
Evaporation	Evaporate

Now using the chain method, link the various processes by using their nicknames (PNN).

VISUALIZATION:

Visualize that you want to separate a mixture into its components, so you open your bedroom **window** and take out your **hand** to pick up the mixture.

Instead of the mixture, you find a **sieve** there.

You see the name **canteen** written on it.

You take it to canteen. There you see a huge **filter machine**.

Now try making further visualization for the above on your own:

_____

_____

_____

_____

Using PNN we can also memorize information like:
Countries–Currencies
Inventors–Inventions
Books–Authors
Minerals–Places
Scientific researches–Scientists
Elements in a periodic table

This is not only useful in day-to-day life, but a must method to be learnt for those appearing in competition exams, where a lot of general knowledge is required. We will talk about it in more detail in the student's section.

We can also memorize vocabulary, difficult words with their meaning, and foreign language words using this technique, which we will see in the next chapter.

CHAPTER AT A GLANCE

❖ Information containing difficult, unfamiliar words or strange names of places and people which are hard to visualize can be memorized using PNN (personal nick name) method.

❖ In this method, we substitute the unknown, difficult word with a familiar sounding word which we can visualize and associate it with the given information.

❖ The substituted word or the nickname can be one word or a group of words.

❖ It is not always necessary to make PNN according to a similar sound of the given word. Any other knowledge or related image can serve as a nick name for that word.

❖ This method is used for memorizing things in general like:
  ➢ Abstract words
  ➢ Technical terms
  ➢ Scientific terminology
  ➢ General facts
  ➢ Names of people and places

❖ Or related to information like:
  ➢ Countries–Currencies
  ➢ Inventors–Inventions
  ➢ Books–Authors
  ➢ Minerals–Places
  ➢ Scientific researches–Scientists
  ➢ Elements in a periodic table
  ➢ Difficult vocabulary with meaning
  ➢ Foreign language words etc.

7

LEARNING FOREIGN LANGUAGE WORDS AND ENGLISH VOCABULARY

Learning a foreign language is the latest trend these days but sometimes it becomes a necessity, like when you are travelling abroad for business or going on a vacation. There are many countries where just knowing English is not enough. In such a scenario, it becomes important for a traveller to learn the local language so that he/she is able to communicate at least basic things like asking for directions, reading a menu card, asking the price for a product etc.

To learn a foreign language, if you follow conventional techniques, it is possible that you will take a few months or even a year to be able to speak in that language.

But here I can teach you a method through which you will be able to master the basics of any given language in as quickly as 10 days! Yes! That's exactly what I mean. In just 10 days!

Though you still need to practice speaking the language to get your grammar and sentence structure correct, most people will agree that their biggest challenge in learning a new language is remembering the new words and their meanings at a good speed without getting confused. We can master a new language words by using the PNN (Personal Nickname) method along with the AIR principle.

MEMORIZING FOREIGN LANGUAGE WORDS

As any word of a foreign language may seem abstract, meaningless, and nonsensical to you, you will not be able to form a mental picture of it. So the first step is to transform a foreign word into a form that is easily understandable and can be visualized in your mind.

For example, let's take a Spanish word like **'cuarto'** which means *'room'*. Now at first glance it will not make sense to someone who is unfamiliar with Spanish language. Therefore, it becomes difficult to visualize it.

If you want to commit this word in your long-term memory so that it becomes easy to recall, you have to transform it into a form that you can easily visualize.

If you speak the word 'cuarto' (pronounced as quart-o) slowly, you will find a familiar and a similar sounding word in it i.e. 'quarter'. Quarter is something meaningful that you can picture in your mind. Now, why not make a ridiculous or illogical association, as you have already learned, between quarter and room?

In Spain, rooms are divided into small quarters.

The next time you try to recall the Spanish word for 'room', your ridiculous association will help you recall quarter, which will further help you recall that the word is 'cuarto'.

Let's take one more example.

In *French*, **'Merci'** means **'Thank you'**.

Just imagine you won a lottery of one lakh rupees and you go to temple or church to thank God. Imagine yourself bending in front of God and saying 'Thank God for your "Merci".'

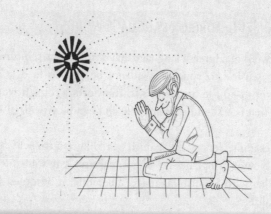

Let's try to remember these five **French words**:

	English word	French word	PNN (nickname)	Image (funny)
1.	Horse	*Chevel*	*Shovel*	A **horse** is digging with a **shovel**.
2.	Money	*Argent*	*Urgent*	It's **urgent** to take out **money** from the bank, so you are rushing towards the bank ATM. *See figure F(a), given on the next page*

	English word	French word	PNN (nickname)	Image (funny)
3.	Father	*Pere*	*Pear*	**Father** is on diet of **pears** only. *See figure F(b), given on the next page*
4.	Garden	*Jardin*	*Jar + den*	**Garden** is put in a big **jar** and placed in a **den**.
5.	Forei-gner	*Un etran-ger*	*Stranger*	A **foreigner** is dressed in a very funny manner, looking like an absolute **stranger**.

Figure: F(a)

Figure: F(b)

Now let's try to learn a few **Spanish words**:

	English word	Spanish word	PNN (nick-name)	Image (funny)
1.	Pen	*Pluma*	*Plum*	My friend gifted me a very special **pen** on my birthday having a big **plum** on it.
2.	book	*el libro*	*Library*	**The library** is full of **books** of my interest.
3.	Time	*Tiempo*	*Tempo*	A **tempo** is carrying a gigantic **time** piece in it. *See figure S(a), given on the next page.*

	English word	Spanish word	PNN (nick-name)	Image (funny)
4.	Face	*Cara*	*Car*	Spanish girls put a lot of make-up on their **face** while driving a **car**.
5.	Prawn	*la gamba*	*Gum-boot*	As soon as I pick up the **gum boot** to wear, many **prawns** start jumping out of it. *See figure S(b), given on the next page.*

Figure: S(a)

Figure: S(b)

The sample associations given above are those that I might use. It is always best to make up your own pictures. Try this method with any foreign language vocabulary, and you'll be able to memorize the words better and faster and with more retentiveness than you ever could before.

Here are some words from German language. Why don't you try to memorize these by using your imagination?

	English word	German word	PNN (nick-name)	Image (funny)
1.	Vegetable	*Gemuse*		
2.	Water	*Wasser*		
3.	Lady	*Dame*		

| 4. | Please | *Bitte* | | |
| 5. | Sorry | *Traurig* | | |

IMPROVING ENGLISH VOCABULARY

Even though we are familiar with English, sometimes we come across some words that we may have never heard before. Then it becomes difficult for us to comprehend its meaning and usage and they seems like foreign words to us. PNN and AIR principle are not just useful in memorizing foreign language words, they can be used to learn words from the English vocabulary as well. We can just break the difficult word into smaller, familiar sounding words and form an image associating these with the meaning of the word.

For example: let's take the word: **'Excruciate'**. It means *'subject to intense pain or mental stress'*. Now we can read this word as *'a screw she ate.'* To memorize this word, just imagine a lady who is in a lot of pain because of 'a screw she ate'.

Let's consider one more example:

'Transient' means *'short lived or passing'*.

Now let's break the word as tran+si+ent or train+see+ant. So you can imagine an ant crossing the railway track just when a train is about to pass. The train sees the ant just for a second and passes away.

Here are a few words for you to try and memorize using the above method. The first few have been done as examples.

	Word	Meaning	PNN (nickname)	Image (funny)
1.	Acrimoni-ous	*Unfriendly, angry and full of strong, bitter feelings and words*	*a+ cry +money*	A boy is crying bitterly for money. He is very unfriendly and angry and saying bitter words to everyone
2.	Oblit-erate	*Destroy, demolish*	m(ob) + literate	Mob of literate citizens demolishing the school building
3.	Diffident	*Shy/Person without self confidence*	Diffi(cult) + dent	Somebody put a very difficult dent on his car, but he is a person without self-confidence and is too shy to complain about this
4.	Waft	*To pass gently*	Raft	A raft is passing gently in water

	Word	Meaning	PNN (nick-name)	Image (funny)
5.	Labyrinth	*Maze*	Lady+Rin	Lady feels lost as if in a maze, in a supermarket looking for Rin soap
6.	Heed	*Listen to*		
7.	Bigot	*Narrow minded person*		
8.	Superflu-ous	*Unnecessary / More than necessary*		
9.	Gadfly	*Irritating person*		
10.	Jaded	*exhausted*		

I am sure you are able to memorize these words with ease and its meaning gets etched in your memory forever.

MEMORIZING SCIENTIFIC TERMS

This method can be used to memorize scientific terminology as well. For example, a medical student, who has to memorize the names of various bones in the human body, may find trouble with memorizing the names of the wrist bones i.e. **S**caphoid, **L**unate, **T**riquetrium, **P**isiform, **T**rapezium, **T**rapezoid, **C**apate, **H**amate.

Using the PNN method, one can convert difficult names of bones into simple pictures and use the chain or hide-and-seek method to arrange them in a sequence.

Name of the Bones	Nicknames (PNN)
Scaphoid	Scarf + avoid
Lunate	Too late
Triquetrium	Trick + aquarium
Pisiform	PC form (shape)
Trapezium	Trapezium (geometrical shape)
Trapezoid	Trap
Capate	Cap + ate
Hamate	Ham + ate

VISUALIZATION

I **avoid**ed wearing a **scarf** as it was hot outside and I was getting **too late**. I was going to play a **trick** on my friends in an **aquarium**. The aquarium was in **PC form (shape)**. Its entry gate was in the shape of a **trapezium**. Inside I saw a big **trap** where an octopus wearing a **Cap ate** fishes with **ham** and omel**ette**.

In this way, a lot of information related to medicine, science, pharmacy, and other related studies can be made easier using this method, especially for students. Many more examples are given in the students' section later in the book.

Cʜᴀᴘᴛᴇʀ ᴀᴛ ᴀ ɢʟᴀɴᴄᴇ

- ❖ Learning a foreign language is not just a trend but a necessity.

- ❖ By using the PNN method along with the AIR principle we can learn a foreign language in just a few days.

- ❖ When we try to learn the words of a foreign language, it is usually difficult as we cannot associate an image to it.

- ❖ The first step is to convert that word into a form that can be easily visualized.

- ❖ This can be done through PNN. Give a familiar nick name to that word.

- ❖ Now associate this nick name with the word's meaning in English.

- ❖ For example: the Spanish word Cara (which means face in English) can be memorized as:

English word	Spanish word	PNN(nick name)	Image (funny)
Face	Cara	Car	Spanish girls put lot of make-up on their face while driving a car.

- ❖ This method can be used to learn not just a foreign language but to learn difficult English words or scientific terms as well.

For example, the meaning of Obliterate can be memorized as:

Word	Meaning	PNN (nick name)	Image (funny)
Obliterate	Destroy, demolish	m(ob) + literate	A mob of literate citizens demolishing the school building.

❖ Through this method you'll be able to memorize the words better and faster and with more retentiveness.

8

MEMORIZING NAMES AND FACES

Someone asked an old man: 'Even after 70 years,
you still call your wife *Darling…Jaan…Sweety….*
Baby…Honey…Luv…!!!
What is the secret of this love?'
The old man replied: '*I forgot her name 10 years ago…*
…and I'm scared to ask her.'

A person's name is his most prized possession, and there is nothing more pleasing to him than hearing his own name or having it remembered by others.

Although I doubt if any of you are as bad as the person in the anecdote, the most common complaint made by people who consider themselves to be in possession of a poor memory is that they are continually forgetting other people's names. They remember the faces (as mentioned before, images are easy to recall), but the names fail to stick. This can be quite a concern, especially for those who work in an environment where they have to meet new people every day. In case you forget someone's name, he/she might feel offended. Also, it is proven that people who remember names easily develop better personal relationships.

Would it not be an asset for any salesman to remember the names of his customers? Or for a doctor to remember the names of his patients, a lawyer, his clients, etc.? Of course, it would. Though everybody likes to achieve this quality, many fail to remember the names of people that they have met. They will remember having seen the person somewhere, but they are not able to locate the place or recollect their name. Sometimes they also fail to identify the person, because they just do not remember the face. The problem of forgetting names and faces is quite common but thankfully, it can be rectified.

HOW TO REMEMBER NAMES

It is not necessary that people only forget difficult or uncommon names. Most of the times the names are simple, but you are just not able to recollect it when you meet that person. It may be due to the fact that you were not paying enough attention while being introduced to the person or because you didn't interacted much with that person. Here is a method through which you can remember as many names as you want in one day and can retain it for a much longer duration.

There are five simple steps to keep in mind while being introduced to someone for the first time, to remember his/her name forever:

STEP 1: PAY ATTENTION TO THE NAME

The main reason why you are not able to recall someone's name may be because **you didn't hear it correctly** in the first place. So make sure you hear the name clearly. If not, ask the person to repeat it.

If it's an odd-sounding name, you may **ask for the correct spelling and pronunciation as well**. Or try to spell it yourself; the person will correct you if you spell it incorrectly. Don't think that person will be hurt. He will be happy that you are taking interest in him.

Make a remark about the name: Whenever you hear anybody's name for the first time, try to relate it with something good and make a remark on it or you can give that person a compliment as well, especially if the name is not very common or sounds unique. I remember about 5 years ago, I met a person at a stall of a publishing house at the International Book Fair in Delhi. His name was Reyansh. Although I was familiar with the meaning of the word, I hadn't heard it being used as somebody's name before. So I complimented him and said, *'Wow! What a unique name! If I am not mistaken, it means God Vishnu's ansh (part of God Vishnu). Isn't it?'*

'Yes! You are right!' he replied. *'Actually my father's name is Vishnu that is why he named me Reyansh.'*

Because of this conversation, I still remember not just his name but his father's as well. Complimenting someone on his name leaves an impression of that person's face along with his/her name in your mind. Also, it is an effective tool to build interpersonal relations.

STEP 2: CREATE A PICTURE OF THAT NAME IN YOUR MIND

After hearing the name clearly, try to give it a picture in your imagination. There are some names that are already meaningful and you can make a mental picture of it immediately like Gagan, Kamal, Prithvi etc.

Then there are certain names that do not have a clear and obvious meaning but they might remind you of someone else. It may be some famous personality or someone personally known to you. In such cases, you can associate this new person's face with that of someone already known to you.

For example, **James** is a very common name in the US. You can visualize *James* (whom you met just now) posing as *James Bond* with a gun in his hand. Someone with the name **Anil** can be imagined in place of *Anil Kapoor (a Bollywood actor)* running around fighting terrorists like he does in the television series *24*.

In India, **Amit** is a very common name. I am sure you know at least one Amit. Let's assume your younger brother's name is Amit. In case you meet someone with the same name, you can imagine him as your brother.

There is a third category of names that do not have any meaning and do not create any picture in your mind. However, with the use of the *Personal Nick Name method*, a name can always be broken down into simpler familiar words and can be given an image.

For example, a name like **Amolika** can be split as **Amul (butter) + lick**. An image of *a girl licking Amul butter* can be visualized.

I remember when I first met *Mr Swaminathan*, a memory trainer from Mumbai, I could immediately break his name into Swami + nath (Hindi word which means chief or head) and visualize him with a long beard touching his feet because he is the nath (chief) of all Swamis of the world. This helped me recollect his name for the first two-three meetings before it got stored in my long-term memory.

When you go to a party or a business meeting, you are introduced to many people but the introductions are very brief. At the end of the day, even if you remember a few names, you are not able to relate them with the faces of all the people you met that evening. **So it is equally important to associate the names with respective faces.** That is where the next step comes in the picture.

STEP 3: TRY TO SEE AN OUTSTANDING FEATURE OR A DISTINCT PART IN THE PERSON'S FACE

Everybody has a distinct feature on their face that can catch your eye. It can be anything like bushy eyebrows, a mole on the cheek, high cheek bones, broad nose, long nose, wide nostrils, thick lips, thin lips, big eyes, small eyes, lines or creases on the forehead, large ears, small ears, dimples, clefts, moustache, double chin, large mouthed, etc. The idea is when you look for some outstanding feature on a person's face, you are paying more attention, observing and etching his face into your memory.

Below are some sample faces to help identify different facial features in faces:

Patchy Skin   Brushy Eyebrows   Scared Face   Birth Mark

Beautiful Eyes   Rough Hair   Uneven Teeth   Bald

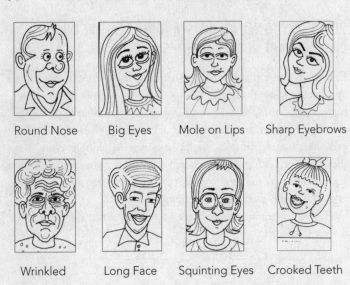

Round Nose   Big Eyes   Mole on Lips   Sharp Eyebrows

Wrinkled   Long Face   Squinting Eyes   Crooked Teeth

STEP 4: ASSOCIATE THE DISTINCT FACIAL FEATURE TO THE PERSON'S NAME

Once you have observed an outstanding feature on the face, you have to now associate the image of the name to that particular feature of the face. For example, let's say you go to a party and meet a pretty girl named *Anjali*. She has big lips. Now we break her name as '*an+jelly*'. You can imagine her applying red jelly on her lips. So whenever you meet her next time, just by looking at her lips, you will be reminded of her name.

OFFICE CRISIS

Let's take one more example:

Suppose four new people are joining your team in office. Your boss introduces them as **Shane, Alisha, Kiran,** and **Balasubramaniam.** How will you remember their names just after a brief introduction?

Let's assume *Shane* has grey eyes. So you can imagine that his grey eyes are shining (Shane) in the dark. Let's move on to *Alisha*. What if she has very thin lips? Think of her name as **'a-little-shy'** and imagine that whenever she looks at you, she gives you **a little shy** smile.

When it comes to **Kiran**, you can break her name into two parts as Key + run. You can imagine that she has a big **key** in her hand and is on the **run**. There is no fixed rule for the association. You can do it in whichever way you want to. You can also associate her with *Kirron Kher*, a famous actress who is also an MP now. Another way of remembering her name is through its meaning. Kiran, in Hindi, means rays of sun. You can visualize that bright rays are emanating from her face.

Suppose Balasubramaniam is bald. As it is a big name, you can break it in three parts as Bala+ super (subra) + money (maniam). And you can imagine that from his bald head, hair (**baal** in hindi) start growing rapidly with **super** big coins (**money**) hanging from them.

It doesn't matter how wild your imagination runs. In fact, the more weird you think, the better will be the recall. As a memory trainer, when people ask me how I memorized their names, sometimes the associated image is so silly that I cannot just share with them what I imagined. So don't worry about it. As long as it is helping you to memorize, it's absolutely fine.

Apart from finding an outstanding feature, there are many other things that can be taken into consideration such as manner of speech, speech defects, character, type of walk, clothing style and so on.

You can also associate a person's name with the kind of work he/she does. For example, you go to a store every week to buy grocery. The name of the lady at the payment counter of the store is **Rosie.** Now, you can imagine that she is standing outside the store, holding a huge bunch of **roses** (Rosie) to welcome you. Next time whenever you see her even at some place other than the store, you can easily recall her image standing at the gate of the store with roses in her hand. This will remind you of not just her name but also the place from where you know her.

STEP 5: REPEAT THE NAME DURING THE COURSE OF YOUR CONVERSATION

It will help you to etch the name more firmly into your mind. Do use the name when you say goodbye or goodnight. At the end of the day, think of each new person you have met and as the names come to mind, jot it down. Next day, go through the list. As you read each person's name, try to see the original association of the name to the face. A picture of the person's face will automatically come to your mind.

Here are a few examples to help you understand the concept more clearly, followed by some names for your practice.

	Names	PNN	Facial features	Visualization (funny)
1.	Samarth	*Sam+(e)arth*	Round Face	Earth (globe) 5 in place of face.
2.	Evelyn	*Evil+in*	Big mouth	Holding a big evil eye in her mouth.
3.	Pandurang	*Paan (beetle leaf)+do+rang (colour)*	Red hair	He is chewing a Paan and doing colour (rang) in his hair.

	Names	PNN	Facial features	Visualization (funny)
4.	Faeem Baig	*Fa+im(in)+bag*	Very fair in complex-ion	She is extremely fair as she always keeps Fa soap in a big bag with her to wash her face often.
5.	Jacob Hill	*Ja+cob Hill*	Pointed nose	A corn Cob instead of his nose sticking out from his face and he is going up hill.
6.	Henry		Bald	
7.	Venkat Srinivas		*Curly hair*	
8.	Shirley		A deep cut on the forehead	
9.	Surekha		Thin lips	
10.	Tripti		Big teeth	

Some more examples of names that can be remembered through PNN are given below for your reference. Do the last few yourself:

	Names	PNN	Visualization (funny)
1.	Krish	*Krishhh...na*	Imagine him as Krishna with a finger on his lips saying 'Shhhh'
2.	Telvin Matthews	*Tell+Win+Math*	Tell me how to win in Math
3.	Ketan Sawalkar	*Chetan+ sawal+kar*	Chetan Bhagat sawal kar raha hai (Chetan Bhagat is asking him questions)
4.	Robin Pedrotti	*Raw+Bin+ paid+roti*	He threw raw bread in the bin and paid for a roti
5.	Oliver Senart	*Olive+se+ art*	Olive se art bana raha hai (he is making an art using Olives)
6.	Christopher fields		
7.	Brian Smith		
8.	Shanker Kukreja		
9.	Sanidhya Swami		
10.	Pedro Fernandes		

I am sure after carefully going through the examples given above; you will be able to do the ones given for practice easily. In case you face some problem, you can refer to the answers below. But always remember, **your own visualization will serve you the best to remember anything and everything.**

Now you are all set to experiment this. Believe in yourself and your ability to remember names.

Meet as many people; just make sure to take interest in their names,

Visualize and associate and you will never forget a single name.

ANSWERS:

	Names	PNN	Facial features	Visualization (funny)
6.	Henry	Hen	Bald	A hen sitting on his bald head
7.	Venkat Srinivas	Cut-wash	*Curly hair*	Just got his long curly hair cut and washed
8.	Shirley	Sir +(Bruce) lee	A deep cut on the forehead	She is fighting with sir Bruce lee and got a deep cut on her forehead which is bleeding
9.	Surekha	Su+rekha (line)	Thin lips	Her lips are as thin as a rekha
10.	Tripti	Trip+teeth	Big teeth	She keeps tripping on her extra long teeth

	Names	PNN	Visualization (funny)
6.	Christopher fields	*Christ-offer-fields*	**Christ** is being **offered fields**
7.	Brian Smith	*Brain-myth*	His brain is a myth
8.	Shanker Kukreja	*Shanker-cook-reja(rajma)*	Shanker ji is cooking rajma
9.	Sanidhya Swami	*Sunny-dhya swami*	On a sunny day she is sitting in dhyan as a swami
10.	Pedro Fernandes	*Petrol-fur-and -dish*	He sold petrol to buy fur and dish

CHAPTER AT A GLANCE

❖ Name is a person's most prized possession and most of us have difficulty in memorizing names of people.

❖ Memory techniques can go a long way in solving this problem.

❖ Steps of memorizing names of people:

1. **Pay attention to the name.**

   ➢ Consider its pronunciation and spelling.
   ➢ Make a remark about it to the person.

2. **Create an image of that name in your mind.**

   ➢ The image can be related to.
   ➢ The meaning of the name.
   ➢ A famous personality with the same name.
   ➢ Someone related to you who share the same name.
   ➢ In case the name does not have a meaning or does not bring an image to your mind you can use PNN method and give it a nick name which can be visualized.

3. **It is important to associate the names with respective faces.** Try and identify any distinct feature in a person's face like bushy eyebrows, a mole on cheek, high cheek bones, long nose, thick lips, big eyes, lines or creases on the forehead, dimples, clefts, moustache, double chin etc.

4. **Associate the distinct facial feature of the person to his/her name.**

5.   **Repeat the name during conversation.**

Points to note:

- ❖ If you did not get the name first time, don't hesitate to ask again.
- ❖ It is not necessary to associate a person's name only with his facial feature. You can relate it with other things like a person's manner of speech, speech defects, character, type of walk, clothing style or the kind of work he/she does.

9

HIDE-AND-SEEK METHOD

In the memory world, this method is known by different names—
**loci method, journey method, placement method, roman room
method,** etc. I like to call it the **hide-and-seek method** because
the method is like a hide-and-seek game being played in our mind
since it involves firstly hiding information to be memorized at
the identified places and then seeking them while recalling from
our imagination. This is probably one of the oldest memory
techniques, used more than 2,000 years ago by Roman orators to
remember the key ideas of their lengthy speeches.

This method can be used not only to memorize points of
speeches, but any list of information in sequence, like checklists,
shopping lists, long sequences of numbers, lengthy answers, etc. It
has many benefits over the chain method which you will understand once you learn the technique.

In the 'Hide-and-Seek' method, we choose a familiar location
or a route in which we identify or mark some stops or places
in a sequence. Then we associate the first item of our list (to be
memorized) with the first stop or mark on our route. I call it
hiding that item in that particular stop in my imagination. While
progressing along the route, we place or hide each item one by one.

For example, if I choose **my drawing room**, then I can decide
some 10 stops in it in a sequence like this:

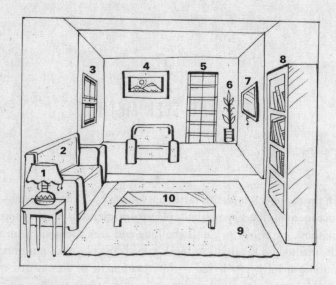

1. *Lamp Shade*
2. *Sofa set*
3. *Window*
4. *Painting*
5. *Door*
6. *Plant*
7. *LED TV*
8. *Book Rack*
9. *Carpet*
10. *Centre Table*

These 10 stops are now my hiding places that I can use to memorize my required information having up to 10 points.

MEMORIZING POINTS OF SPEECH

Do you have the fear of public speaking? If yes, then you are not alone! In fact, it is rated as number one fear of people around the world.

A speech leaves a better impact if the orator presents the points in a flow. Most people prepare for their presentation/speech well and are confident until the time they reach the stage. But once they are up on stage, the situation changes completely.

They become aware of hundreds of eyes looking at them and the fear of forgetting important points seeps in. They usually become quiet or start mumbling, messing up a well-prepared speech. Unfortunately, this leaves a bad impression on their psyche and they feel more tense the next time they face an audience. Luckily, there's a simple fix. All you need is a little time and the right technique!

Now let's say I have to memorize a *speech* on '*Qualities of a Good Leader*', and the points to remember are:

- Honest
- Disciplined
- Healthy
- Dedicated
- Punctual
- Good Communication Skills
- Cooperative
- Caring
- Motivating
- Encouraging

Now to memorize the above points, just try to visualize them by using the PNN method and then associate these qualities with each of the stops in the drawing room in a sequence. Let's see how you can do it:

1. **Honest:** Visualize a *nest* (honest) on the **lampshade**.

2. **Disciplined:** A **sofa** set is loaded with lots of flying discs (disciplined).

3. **Healthy:** Packets of *healthy food like oats* cereals are hanging from the **window.**

4. **Dedicated:** I am praising a **painting** of *daddy* (dedicated) on the wall.

5. **Punctual:** I am giving a solid *punch* (punctual) to the **door** to break it open.

6. **Good communication skills:** A **plant** starts *communicating* with me.

7. **Co-operative:** An *operation* (co-operative) is being done in the **TV** show.

8. **Caring:** Many toy cars (caring) are placed on the **book rack.**

9 **Motivating:** A *moti* (fat woman) is weighing herself standing on the **carpet.**

10. **Encouraging:** An *anchor* (encouraging) is standing with a mike on the **centre table.**

Now after visualizing the points like this, while delivering the speech, just imagine the stops of drawing room sequentially in your mind and the points can be recalled very confidently.

Checking Point:

While visualizing the stops of a drawing room in your mind, try to recall and write all the qualities of good leader in the same sequence in the table given below:

1. _____

2. _____

3. _____

4. _____

5. _____

6. _____

7. _____

8. _____

9. _____

10. _____

There are many locations, routes, and places in your mind from which you need to look for some hide-and-seek places that you will require to memorize information.

RULES TO IDENTIFY OR CREATE HIDE-AND-SEEK PLACES

While creating the list of '*Hide-and-Seek*' places, remember the following key points:

❖ The location should be a familiar one, like your own room or house or a familiar route such as the route to your school/office, or a route you take for a shopping mall, etc. It should be a route that never changes and that is already present in your memory.

❖ While making the list of stops in a particular room, take distinct items as stops. For example, don't take 2 paintings on the same wall or two chairs in the same room as 2 different stops. The hiding places should be unique so that when we try to seek (recall) the information, we should not get confused.

❖ The stops or places must be in a sequence, otherwise we might lose some information while recalling, if we miss any of the stops.

Let's create another *hide-and-seek* route keeping the above points in mind. Suppose following are the stops in sequence when you enter my office building:

1. Gate
2. Guard room
3. Parking
4. Biometric reader
5. Reception
6. Conference room
7. Lift
8. Accounts department
9. Manager's room
10. Secretary's room
11. My own cubicle
12. Cafeteria

This is a list of stops in sequence at my office. You can create your own list according to your route.

MEMORIZING ZODIAC SIGNS IN A SEQUENCE

I really had a hard time in my teenage years memorizing all 12 zodiac signs in the right sequence. But now it's all so easy. You can do it on the first reading. Here is the list of zodiac signs.

Aries

Taurus

Gemini

Cancer

Leo

Virgo

Libra

Scorpio

Sagittarius

Capricorn

Aquarius

Pisces

We will associate each zodiac sign with the above hiding places (of office) using the PNN method:

S. No.	Hiding places / Route	Zodiac Signs	PNN	Visualization
1.	Gate	Aries	Air Balloons	*Gate* is made up of multicolored *air balloons*
2.	Guard Room	Taurus	Tall Rusk	*Guard* is eating a *long rusk* that is as *tall* as him
3.	Parking	Gemini	Gems	Everyone is getting a *gem* as a *parking* token
4.	I.D. Checking	Cancer	Cancer (disease)	Everyone is being checked for cancer
5.	Reception	Leo	Leo toys	Lady at reception is selling Leo toys here

S. No.	Hiding places / Route	Zodiac Signs	PNN	Visualization
6.	Conference room	Virgo	Where to go	People are standing outside the conference room wondering where to go
7.	Lift	Libra	Library	There is a huge library in the lift
8.	Accounts department	Scorpio	Scorpions	Scorpions are jumping over the accountant's head
9.	Manager's room	Sagittarius	Sage	The manager has become a sage
10.	Secretary's room	Capricorn	Capri with corns	The secretary is wearing a capri with corns growing on it
11.	My cubicle	Aquarius	Aquarium	There is an aquarium on my seat in my cubicle
12.	Cafeteria	Pisces	Dices	Everyone is sitting on big dices in cafeteria

Though these things are actually not present at these places in reality, you can think as if you have hidden them in these places in your imagination. So whenever you pass a manager's room it will remind you of him disguised as a sage, which will further remind you of the zodiac sign Sagittarius.

Similarly, when you will visualize the lift in your imagination, a picture of a big library in the lift will come to your mind, which further will remind you of the zodiac sign Libra. As soon as you visualize the next place, i.e. accounts department, you can easily see the scorpions jumping over the accountant's head in your imagination, which will help you recall that the next zodiac sign is Scorpio.

In this way, when you will visualize your hiding places in office in that particular sequence in your mind, it will help you to recall all 12 zodiac signs in sequence.

MEMORIZING A CHECKLIST

Now, make a sequence of hiding places in any one of your familiar route with at least 10 stops. Name the route first, i.e. the location you chose, and then write 10 places or stops in that route. The route can be the way you take to your school or office or your own house or it can be the route from your house to your office or to a local market, where different shops can serve as hiding places as well.

1. _____

2. _____

3. _____

4. _____

5. _____

6. _____

7. _____

8. _____

9. _____

10. _____

Repeat it once in your mind.

Now try to remember the following **list of things you require** for checking before going on a vacation.

- Gas and all lights switched off
- Tickets
- I-cards
- Passports
- Medicines
- Food items
- Money
- All luggage
- Mobile and charger
- House keys

Now associate your list items one by one with the hiding places in your route and memorize them by visualizing them.

Visualizing your journey *(of hiding places)*, try to recall your checklist.

I am sure you will be able recall the above information using your new journey.

After practicing the above exercises, you can easily remember 10 things by associating them with 10 places in your room or route. But what if you have to memorize a list of 20, 30, or even more words or items? In that case, either you can find more places in the same room or you can use three or more rooms to create a list of 30 or more hiding places if required. You can always add more locations on your route or journey.

I am sure you will be able recall the above information using your new journey.

After practicing the above exercises, you can easily remember 10 things by associating them with 10 places in your room or route. But what if you have to memorize a list of 20, 30, or even more words or items? In that case, either you can find more places in the same room or you can use three or more rooms to create a list of 30 or more hiding places if required. You can always add on locations on your route or journey.

This method is the most reliable one among all memory techniques and is mostly used by memory champions all over the world.

I also made my **national record of memorizing 210 binary digits** in just 146 seconds using this technique along with the number peg system that we will discuss in the following chapters.

One of my students, *Ekta*, also made a **national record of memorizing 507 words** in a sequence after hearing them just once using this technique.

BENEFITS OF THE HIDE-AND-SEEK METHOD

➤ The beauty of this method is that you can have unlimited hiding places using which you can memorize unlimited amount of information. You can create new hiding places wherever you go on a daily basis.

➤ This method scores more over other methods as even if you are not able to recall information on any one of the stops, you can still continue recalling from the next stop. The sequence is not disturbed.

CHAPTER AT A GLANCE

❖ *'Hide-and-seek'* method is the most reliable memory technique and is used by almost all memory champions of the world.

❖ It is also known by different names such as loci method, journey method, placement method, roman room method, etc.

❖ In the *'Hide-and-seek'* method, we choose a familiar location or a route in which we identify some stops or places in a sequence.

❖ Then we associate items to be memorized with these stops.

❖ Hiding places should be familiar and unique.

❖ Stops must be in a sequence.

❖ This method can be used to memorize things like:

  ➢ Points of speech

  ➢ Answers

  ➢ Shopping lists

  ➢ Minutes of meetings

  ➢ Checklists

  ➢ And much more information which is in a sequence or points form.

10

MNEMONICS

Mnemonics (pronounced 'new-mon-ics') are methods, devices, or any learning techniques that helps in retention of information. The word comes from the Greek word '**mnemonikós**', which means 'of memory or relating to memory'.

Ancient Greeks and Romans distinguished between two types of memory: the 'natural' memory and the 'artificial' memory. The former is inborn, and is the one that everyone uses automatically and without thinking. Artificial memory in contrast has to be trained and developed through learning and practicing a variety of mnemonic techniques. There are studies done in the past that prove students who regularly use mnemonics show a remarkable increase in their test scores.

But mnemonics aren't just for children. In an article titled 'Stalking the Wild Mnemos: Research That's Easy to Remember', educational psychologist Joel R. Levin concluded that '*sufficient research evidence now exists to suggest that even skilled learners can become more skilled through mnemonic strategy acquisition and implementation*'.

FORMS OF MNEMONICS

Mnemonics are of various forms like:

➤ Rhyme mnemonics
➤ Acronyms

➤ Acrostics
➤ Music Mnemonics
➤ Number Phrase Mnemonics
➤ Image Mnemonics and
➤ Spelling Mnemonics

1. RHYME MNEMONICS

In this form of Mnemonics, the given information is transformed into a poem.

For example: Do you remember when Columbus sailed to America?

In Fourteen-hundred ninety-two, Columbus sailed the ocean blue.

Wouldn't it be easy to recall now?

A commonly used **Rhyme Mnemonic** for the number of days in each month is:

30 days hath September, April, June, and November.
All the rest have 31,
Except February, my dear son.
It has 28 and that is fine,
But in Leap Year it has 29.

Similarly, mnemonic for memorizing the year in which **three new states named Chattisgarh, Uttarakhand, and Jharkhand** were formed in India could be:

2000 was the date,
When India got three new states.
Chattisgarh, Uttarakhand,
And then followed Jharkhand.

The three Battles of Panipat can be memorized as
The first battle of Panipat,

1526 was when it was fought.
Thirty years later(1556) again it happened,
That was Panipat battle number second.
1761 was battle number third,
Which was won by Ahmad.

If you learn things like this, you will be able to remember it for a longer period of time. Adding a rhyme to any given text adds to its recall value.

2. ACRONYM *(First Letter Mnemonic)*

In this, the first letter from a list of words is taken to form a new word. That new word is called an **Acronym**. Acronyms are used in many fields.

Some common acronyms you must be aware of are:

➢ UNO: United Nations Organization
➢ LASER: Light Amplification by Stimulated Emission of Radiation
➢ AIDS: Acquired Immunedeficiency Syndrome
➢ ATM: Automated Teller Machine

We can make our own acronyms by taking the first letter of each word in a list of items to be remembered which can serve as a mnemonic. This is especially useful when you have to remember a short list of words in a particular order.

For example, in my childhood, my mother made me remember the seven colours of the rainbow by using the word **VIBGYOR** which involves the first letter of seven colours in a sequence (Violet, Indigo, Blue, Green, Yellow, Orange, Red).

I also used this technique in the beginning of the book to introduce you to the three laws of memory by forming the word *AIR*.

AIR: Association, **I**magination, **R**idiculous Thinking

Just by remembering the word AIR, you will be able to recall the three laws easily.

Some other examples of learning through Acronyms are:

> **PEDMAS**—To remember the order of functions to solve an algebraic equation in Mathematics: **P**arentheses, **E**xponents, **D**ivision, **M**ultiplication, **A**ddition, and **S**ubtraction.

> **HOMES**—To remember the Great Lakes of North America: **H**uron, **O**ntario, **M**ichigan, **E**rie, **S**uperior.

> **FANBOYS**—To remember the coordination conjunctions in English: *for, and, nor, but, or, yet, so.*

> **PVT.TIM HALL**—Essential amino acids: **P**henylanine, **V**aline, **T**hreonine, **T**ryptophan, **I**solucine, **M**ethionine, **H**istidine, **A**rginine, **L**eucine, **L**ysine.

> **BHAJSAB**—To remember the rulers from the Mughal dynasty-**B**abar, **H**umayun, **A**kbar, **J**ehangir, **S**hahjahan, **A**urangzeb, and **B**ahadur Shah Zafar.

When it is not necessary to remember the information in a sequence, the letters can be rearranged to make a more meaningful word. For example, ***body's excretory organs*** are **Liver, Kidneys, Skin, Lungs, and Intestines.** The initials are **LKSLI** which can be rearranged to form a meaningful word **SKILL.** Now you can easily relate it by saying that body has a ***skill*** *to excrete* wastes. It's important to connect or associate the acronym with the topic of the information to be learnt (in this case, excretory organs).

CAUTION: While making new words, it is important that you are familiar with the words whose initials you are using. For example, you must know the names of the great lakes of North America, and only then will the acronym HOMES be useful to you. If you don't know the names, then other methods like the PNN and chain method can be more useful.

3. ACROSTICS *(First Letter Sentence Mnemonic)*

In this form of Mnemonic, the first letter of each term is taken and starting from those letters, some new words are formed in such a way that they make a meaningful sentence. This is the most commonly used mnemonic popularly known as **Acrostics**. Such mnemonics are generally used when you have to memorize a list of items in a specific order.

For example:

Planets	The order of planets according to their distance from the Sun: Mercury, Venus, Earth, Mars, Jupiter, Saturn, Uranus, Neptune
Acrostic	**My Very Educated Mother Just Served Us Noodles**
Oceans	Oceans of the world: Indian, Arctic, Atlantic, Pacific
Acrostic	**I Am At Peace**
Zodiac Signs	Aries, Taurus, Gemini, Cancer, Leo, Virgo, Libra, Scorpio, Sagittarius, Capricorn, Aquarius, Pisces
Acrostic	**As The Great Cook Likes Very Little Spice, She Carefully Adds Pepper**

In this particular case, where two zodiac signs, Leo and Libra are starting with letter 'L', a person may mistakenly relate 'Likes' with Libra instead of Leo. To avoid that misunderstanding, one can make an association with the spelling of the two. Leo has 'e' after L and Libra has 'i' after L and since e comes before i in alphabet, so Leo comes before Libra in zodiac signs.

Continents	Europe, Antarctica, Asia, Africa, Australia, North America, South America
Acrostic	Eat An Aspirin After A Night Snack In the above example, as letter A is repeated, we have taken the first two letters of the words to differentiate.
Carpal Bones	Scaphoid, Lunate, Triquetral, Pisiform, Trapezium, Trapezoid, Capitate, Hamate
Acrostic	Some Loving Teachers Play Tennis To Create Harmony Or She Looks Too Pretty, Try To Catch Her
Seven levels of thinking ability	Recall, Translation, Interpretation, Application, Analysis, Synthesis, Evaluation
Acrostic	Road To Intelligence Allows Ample Space for Exercise
Seven Qualities of Soul	Bliss, Knowledge, Peace, Love, Happiness, Purity, and Power

Acrostic	Benign King Peter Loved Honouring People Power

The **Music world** has long made use of mnemonics to help students in remembering the orders of notes. There are many fine examples; I will list a few.

- ➢ *FACE*— The order of the spaces in the treble clef.
- ➢ *All Cows Eat Grass* (ACEG)—The order of the spaces in the bass clef.

And then one for memorizing all the various types of scales:

- ➢ I Don't Play Like My Aunt Lilly

  (Ionian, Dorian, Phrygian, Lydian, Mixolodian, Aeolian, Locrian)

4. MUSIC MNEMONICS

There is a popular belief that learning and remembering information can be enhanced by setting the information to music. In a country like India, where hundreds of movies are released in a year and each movie has an average of 4 songs, music plays a very important part in our lives. Advertisements on radio and TV use music to help potential customers remember their products when shopping. It has been noticed that with sufficient repetition of ads, the shopper starts reciting an oft-repeated phrase from the commercial or starts singing the lyrics of the promotion melody. This has resulted in increased sales of the product.

The most recent example is of the new advt. of 'Honda' in which the brand is promoted through a song *'Dekho dekhe yeh zamana…'* This song has a great recall value not just with grown-ups but with kids. As soon as they hear this song, they know it's a 'Honda' ad.

Some other examples of famous advertisement slogans are:

Amul	:	*Utterly butterly delicious! Amul!*
Cadbury	:	*Kuch meetha ho jaaye!*
L'oreal	:	*Because you're worth it!*
McDonalds	:	*I am loving it!*
Thumbs Up	:	*Taste the thunder!*
Siyaram	:	*Come home to Siyaram.*

Did You Know ???

From the time we are two-years-old, we learn how to memorize things by singing mnemonics, *For example*, everybody knows the ABC song! We learn to memorize ABC at a very young age. According to an online survey at squidoo.com, when memorizing the ABCs, 67 percent used the ABC song, 12 percent memorized it with a rhyme, while 7 percent with no rhyme or song and just with flashcards.

By putting a simple melody to the ABCs, we were all able to memorize twenty-six letters in no time, that too at such a young age! So why can't we use this technique while memorizing when we are older?

In India, it is a common trend to compose devotional songs to the tunes of popular Bollywood numbers. Has it ever happened with you that while listening to that devotional song, the original song comes to your mind? You can recall the exact lyrics of the original song just by hearing its tune. Similarly, in case you have to memorize a lot of text in a short time, you can put it as lyrics of your most favourite song and sing it over and over again. So whenever you will think of the original song, the new lyrics will come to your mind.

WHAT TO LEARN? SING ALONG!

Disney even caught on to the idea of teaching through song in an episode of 'Hannah Montana' released in 2007. In the episode, Miley must learn bones of the human body in order to pass her midterm exams. In order to do this, she figures out that it's easiest to memorize them if she puts them in place of the words of one of her songs.

You can search it on internet by typing 'Hannah Montana Bone dance.' Or watch its video on youtube using the following address: https://www.youtube.com/watch?v=ZGdK4T7WUrA

You may also read its lyrics using the following address:

http://www.lyricsmode.com/lyrics/h/hannah_montana/the_bone_dance.html

5. NUMBER PHRASE TECHNIQUE

It is generally considered easier to remember words, especially when they are associated with another object in some meaningful way, than it is to recall random numbers. Numbers are usually difficult to visualize as well. Number mnemonics can be used to memorize information like addresses, invoice numbers, phone extension etc.

In this method, you have to convert numbers in words to make a phrase that is easy to remember.

For example, your friend's **house number is 134.** To memorize it you have to think of a one-letter word, then a three-letter word, and then a four-letter word. But you have to keep in mind that after putting it together, it should become a phrase. Like:

I	Say	Open
1	3	4

Now if your friend's name is Ronit, just imagine you are banging the door of his house and saying *'I Say Open'*. This way you will remember that this phrase is related to Ronit's address.

You can also use this method to memorize telephone extensions. Example: Your father's extension number in office is **2625**. You can memorize it as.

My	Father	Is	Funny
2	6	2	5

To memorize a big number like the customer Id of your bank account, you can create a phrase.

Let's assume the number is 2525249. You can memorize it as:

My	Money	Is	saved	In	Bank	Carefully
2	5	2	5	2	4	9

But in the above example, if there is 0 instead of 9, then how will you do it? Can you create a word that has zero letters in it? No. In such a case, you can form a 10-letter word and consider it as a substitute for zero. The new phrase for 2525240 will be:

My	Money	Is	lying	In	Bank	Carelessly
2	5	2	5	2	4	0

Suppose an address is a combination of letters and numbers, then you can make phrases that include those letters E.g. an address like: M-5/ A-4: can be remembered as:

M	Tells	A	Joke
M	5	A	4

You can imagine a big letter M is telling a joke to the person whose address you are trying to memorize.

PRACTICE MAKES PERFECT

Using the above technique try to remember the following details.

	Number	Phrase	Association
Passport			
IFSC code of your bank			

Besides this, there are some other very unique pegging methods to memorize numbers which we will discuss in the next two chapters.

IMAGE MNEMONICS

It is a well-established fact that our mind easily remembers images. The advantage of imagining is that it provides an easy way of connecting information that is not readily connected otherwise. Using imagery can make learning more fun and interesting. Image mnemonics techniques generally involve two tasks:

➢ Forming mental images
➢ Making association between images.

The techniques that you learnt in the previous chapters like Chain method, PNN and Hide-and-Seek are basically different form of image mnemonics.

Just to remind you about these techniques, let's take an example. Suppose you want to memorize the currency of Russia that is Ruble.

You can remember it by using the PNN method imagining that *'Because of **rushing** you fell into the **rubble**'*
(Russia: Rush, Ruble: rubble)

When you start applying these techniques in your day-to-day life, you will realize that many a times you are using more than one method to memorize the given information. That is absolutely fine!

Just as in case of a car. You can't drive it only with a steering or with wheels or with just an oil tank. All these things need to be assembled together for you to drive it. Similarly, you can pick and choose more than one technique to memorize whatever information is required. With practice, you will soon master all these techniques.

Since many children as well as adults also find difficulty in memorizing spellings, spelling mnemonics are discussed in detail in the next chapter separately.

CHAPTER AT A GLANCE

❖ *Mnemonics are methods or devices that help in retention of information.*

❖ *Forms of mnemonics.*

> **Rhyme mnemonics**: In this we convert the given information in the form of a poem so that it becomes easy and interesting to memorize.

  E.g; *In Fourteen-hundred ninety-two, Columbus sailed the ocean blue.*

> **Acronyms:** Here first letter from the list of words is taken to form a new word.

  E.g; AIDS: **A**cquired **I**mmune **D**eficiency **S**yndrome

> **Acrostic:** In this, the first letter of each term is taken to form such words that make a meaningful sentence. E.g: Oceans of the world: **I**ndian, **A**rctic, **A**tlantic, **P**acific can be remembered as '*I am At Peace'.*

> **Music Mnemonics:** We associate the given information with music by infusing a melody to it. Jingles in advertising or nursery rhymes like ABC are some examples.

> **Number Phrase Mnemonics:** In this we choose a two letter word for number 2 and a three letter word for number 3, and so on. With these words we make a meaningful phrase to remember the number. This method can be used to memorize:

❖ Addresses

❖ Invoice numbers

❖ Phone extn.

❖ IFSC code of banks
❖ Customer ID numbers etc.
  ➢ **Image Mnemonics:** Here we visualize any given information in the form of an image and then associate various images to memorize the complete information. PNN, Hide-and-Seek and Chain method are examples of Image mnemonics.
  ➢ **Spelling Mnemonics:** This form of mnemonic is used to memorize spellings of various simple as well as complex words.

11

MEMORIZING SPELLINGS

SPELLING MNEMONICS

When it comes to spellings, English can be a very tricky language. Lots of words have letters that are silent or two words might have the same sound but different spellings. There are certain words in which a particular letter is repeated a number of times. That makes it really confusing and in case you miss one letter, it changes the complete meaning of the word. Spelling mnemonics is intended to help us to correctly remember spellings of all kind of words.

For example :

✦ **Believe or Beleive**

Many people find it confusing whether the spelling has 'ie' or 'ei'. The correct spelling is *Believe.* Just remember it by the phrase: 'Never Be*lie*ve a *Lie*'
Now whenever you will write the word *Believe, 'lie'* will automatically come to your mind.

✦ **Argument or Arguement**

Argument: To spell it, remember the phrase:
I lost an 'e' in an 'Argument'?

❖ **Ascertain or Accertain**

Ascertain: When you ascertain a fact, be AS CERTAIN as you possibly can

❖ **Business or Bussiness**

Business: There is a **Bus**iness meeting going on inside a **Bus**

Some more examples:

❖ *Slaughter:* LAUGHTER with an 'S' in the beginning.

❖ *Embarrass:* Can you spell it correctly without missing a single 'r' or 's'? Well, remember it as follows:

'I go really red when my sister sings'.

❖ **Mississippi: Miss is sipp**ing tea in Mississippi.

❖ **Separate:** has a '**rat**' in it –sep- a- rat-e

❖ **Stationery:** *'e'* for envelope, which means the other stationary *(not moving)* is the one with the *'a'* in it.

❖ **Necessary:** In the word **Necessary**, confusion is in the number of Cs and Ss.
You can remember it through a phrase: 'It's necessary to have **one** cup of tea with **two** sugars.'

Spellings can also be memorized using ACROSTICS

For example, *necessary* can also be learnt by saying:

❖ **N**ever **E**at **C**risps, **E**at **S**alad **S**andwiches, **A**nd **R**emain **Y**oung!
❖ *Ocean:* **O**nly **C**at's **E**yes **A**re **N**arrow
❖ *Rhythm:* **R**hythm **H**elps **Y**our **T**wo **H**ips **M**ove
❖ *Geography:* **G**eorge's **E**lderly **O**ld **G**randfather **R**ode **A** **P**ig **H**ome **Y**esterday

- *Arithmetic*: A Rat In The House May Eat The Ice Cream
- *Laugh*: Little Anger Upsets Good Health (so keep laughing)

Acrostics will help you not only to remove the confusion in spelling; it will also help you memorize the complete spelling of the word. You need to use the complete sentence just for a few times initially. With regular use of the word, the correct spelling will get embedded in your long-term memory and you won't have to remember the complete phrase later.

WORDS WITH THE SAME SOUND BUT DIFFERENT SPELLINGS

- *Affect and Effect*

  Affect describes an action and effect is the end consequence.

  You can also remember it with the word RAVEN:

  Remember

  Affect (is)

  Verb

  Effect (a)

  Noun

- *Desert and Dessert*

  Remember a Desert is 's'andy and dessert is too (two) sweet with two 'S'.

- *Hear/Here*

  You Hear with your EAR

❖ *Principal (of a school) and Principle (a rule)*

A princi**pal** at a school is your **pal**, and a princip**le** you believe or follow is a ru**le**.

Some more tips for better spellings:

1. This may be the best-known spelling rule:

   i before *e,* except after *c* or when sounded like 'ay' as in *neighbour* and *weigh*

   Here are some words that follow the rule:

   IE words: *believe, field, relief*

   CEI words: *ceiling, deceit, receive*

   EI words: *freight, reign, sleigh*

   Some exceptions: *either, foreign, height, leisure, protein, weird*

   'CIEN words' are another exception to the rule. These include *ancient, efficient,* and *science.*

2. Have you heard the expression:

   'When two vowels go walking, the first one does the talking?'

   This means that when there are two vowels in a row, the first usually has a long sound and the second is silent. That's why the word 'Team' is pronounced as 'Teem' where 'a' is silent. Similarly *coat,* not *caot;* and *wait,* not *wiat.* Remembering this rule will help you to put vowels in the right order.

3. Find words within the word.

   ➢ When: There is 'hen' in 'when'

   ➢ What: has a 'hat' in it

4. Break the word up into sounds:

   ➢ Complementary: comp–le–ment–ary

   ➢ Wednesday: Wed–nes–day

➢ February: Feb–r–u–ary

➢ Saturday: Sat–ur–day

➢ Friend: Fri + end

➢ Lovely: Love + ly

5. Write the confusing letter extra large in size:

➢ Let's take a word 'repetitious'. Many people write it as repititious, You can remember that it is 'e' not 'i' by making that 'e' stand out from the rest by writing it extra large ('rep-E-titious'). Look at it and concentrate on it for a moment. Chances are you will spell it correctly from here onwards.

➢ Liquefy: liqu-E-fy

6. Write the word with your finger in the air, or in sand. Or you may write the spelling in big writing on a piece of paper and then trace over the letters with the finger several times, repeating the sounds. It helps to have a better impression in the mind by combining kinesthetic, auditory, and verbal input.

7. *Count the letters: If you remember that there are 13 letters in 'accommodation', you are more likely to include the double letters.*

These are a few examples of confusing words of different kinds whose spellings can be memorized using different kinds of associations. Now whenever you find any difficult or confusing word, observe the spelling carefully. I am sure you will be able to find some or the other association to retain it in your memory.

CHAPTER AT A GLANCE

❖ **Spelling mnemonics** helps us to remember the spellings of words correctly.

❖ We can also use various associations to memorize long and tricky words.
   For example, for memorizing the spelling of necessary, if you have confusion in the number of Cs and Ss, you can remember it through a phrase: 'It's necessary to have **one c**up of tea with **two s**ugars.'

❖ If you are confused which vowel out of 'e' and 'a' comes first and how many times, you can remember it through a phrase: '**e**at **e**astern apples'. Furthermore, you can also relate this phrase with the word necessary by saying 'It's necessary to eat eastern apples to have a good memory'.

❖ If you want to memorize the complete spelling of necessary, you can do it by using an acrostic: **N**ever **E**at **C**risps, **E**at **S**alad **S**andwiches, **A**nd **R**emain **Y**oung!

So there are various ways to fix a spelling in your memory—it depends on where you are getting confused and what association works best for you.

1 2

PEG SYSTEM

Just as a physical hook on a wall can help you to hang something on it, in the same way, a mental hook or a 'peg' can help you hold information in your mind. We have already learnt that any new information can be stored in the brain by connecting it with any existing information. That old information serves as **pegs** for the new one. Information like **counting numbers** *(say 1 to 20)* or **alphabets** *ABC* that we know well since our childhood can serve as pegs to associate any new information.

Since numbers are abstract, intangible, and difficult to visualize, *how can we associate numbers with things to remember?* So here we are going to share a few methods that will help you convert numbers into images.

We call this the 'Number Rhyme Method'.

NUMBER RHYME METHOD

Rhyme method is a very useful, yet simple and powerful peg system used to memorize list information. It not only allows you to remember items in their correct order, but also the item's exact position on the list.

In this method, we represent numbers by images of things that rhyme with it.

Here is a chart of images we can assign to the numbers according to their rhyming sound:

1 ONE	SUN	2 TWO	SHOE
3 THREE	TREE	4 FOUR	DOOR
5 FIVE	HIVE	6 SIX	TICKS
7 SEVEN	LEMON	8 EIGHT	PLATE
9 NINE	LINE	10 TEN	HEN

These are the images that I use. You can choose rhyming items for each number as per your liking. For example, number **one** can be visualized as *bun* or *nun* or *gun* also. Similarly, besides *shoe*, number **two** can be visualized as *glue*.

> *Caution:* The images that you choose for the numbers should be concrete ones, not abstract. For example, number three can be *tree or sea*, but not *free* as visualizing free is a bit difficult compared to other two.

PRACTICE MAKES PERFECT

Try to recall the rhyme images given in the above chart and complete the following table:

Three   =   _____

Six   =   _____

Two   =   _____

Ten   =   _____

Seven   =   _____

One   =   _____

Four   =   _____

Nine   =   _____

Five   =   _____

Eight   =   _____

Now, you can use these number rhymes to memorize a list of 10 items in order by connecting the pegs with the items you want to remember. With a little bit of practice, you can memorize any list of 10 items between one to two minutes. What's more, the memory for the list tends to be a lot stronger than if you had used rote learning.

MEMORIZING INGREDIENTS OF A RECIPE

Suppose you visit a friend one evening and she serves you an apple pie. You love it and ask her for the ingredients that she has used. She tells you a list of 8 ingredients but as you are not carrying a pen, you decide to memorize it. Let's see how you will memorize this list using peg system.

1. Apples
2. Sugar
3. Flour
4. Butter
5. Essence
6. Egg
7. Lemon juice
8. Milk

Visualization:

Peg for number one is sun, To remember the first item in the list, i.e. apples, make an association of sun with apple. Similarly, rhyming peg for two is shoe, so associate shoe with item number 2, i.e. sugar.

Likewise, you can imagine all the items with their rhyming pegs as follows:

1. A big bright *sun (one)* is shining on a huge **apple**.
2. Imagine a shining blue coloured *shoe (two)* is full of **sugar**.
3. Visualize a big *tree (three)* is shedding **flour** on everybody who sits under it.

4. Imagine that you are closing a *door (four)* and the knob of the door is made up of butter and your hand is slipping on it.

5. Now imagine that all the bees are collecting **essence** in their *hive (five)*.

6. For eggs you can visualize yourself breaking the **eggs** with a thick and long *stick (six)*.

7. Visualize lemon juice being squeezed from a big *lemon (seven)*.

8. And last you can imagine you are drinking **milk** from a *plate (eight)*.

MEMORIZING APPOINTMENTS

As you can now *visualize* numbers through rhyme images, you can remember anything related to numbers as well. Earlier you learn to remember list of things to do using chain or hide and seek method, but using number rhyme method, we will now be able to remember the appointments along with time. Let's say, on a particular Saturday, you have the following schedule:

TIME	APPOINTMENT/THINGS TO DO
9 am	Call to boss
10am	Parents–teacher meeting (PTM)
11am	Shopping
1pm	Lunch with an old friend
3 pm	Meeting a client in a café
5 pm	Appointment with dentist

TIME	APPOINTMENT/THINGS TO DO
6 pm	Taking kids to dance class
7 pm	Picking up a dress from a boutique
8 pm	Going to watch a movie

To memorize the above appointments, we need some more rhyming images like for number 11. We can extend the number rhyme method chart for numbers from 11 to 20 as shown below:

11 ELEVEN	 HEAVEN	**12** TWELVE	 SHELF
13 THIRTEEN	 THIRSTING	**14** FOURTEEN	 FOUR TINS

15 FIFTEEN	 LIFTING	**16** SIXTEEN	 SWEET SIXTEEN
17 SEVEN- TEEN	 CANTEEN	**18** EIGHTEEN	 ACHING
19 NINETEEN	 KNIGHT	**20** TWENTY	 AUNTY

Now you don't want to get confused whether your appointment with the doctor is at 4 pm or 5 pm. You want to be sure that you do remember all the things on time. One way is to write it down, but after writing, if we can give just one more minute's time to keep it in mind, then it would be an added advantage and we do not have to see the list again and again.

Visualization for Appointments:

1. **9 am:** Visualize you are standing in **line** to call your *boss*.
2. **10 am:** A **hen** is sitting in place of the teacher during *PTM*.
3. **11 am:** You are going to **heaven** for *shopping*.
4. **1 pm:** Visualize yourself having *lunch with your friend* under the **sun**.
5. **3 pm:** Visualize yourself climbing a **tree** with your *client to reach a café* on top of the tree.
6. **5 pm:** *The dentist* is taking honey from a **hive** into his clinic and putting it on your tooth.
7. **6 pm:** Visualize *kids are dancing* on long **sticks** tied to their feet.
8. **7 pm:** Your *dress* has **lemons** hanging all over it as it is a latest fashion trend.
9. **8 pm:** You are *watching a movie* sitting on a big **plate** instead of a seat.

Visualize these associations clearly in your mind. Try to recall them without looking at the list.

What were you suppose to do at 3 o'clock?

We are sure 3 will remind you of a tree; *what can you see in your imagination, on a tree? ...*

If you had done the visualization as given above, you will surely recall yourself climbing on to a tree with your client to reach the café on the top of the tree. Or if we ask you the time of the kids' dance class, then immediately the image of kids dancing on sticks will further remind you that it is at six.

Tip: The weirder the visualization, the better is the recall. So do not hesitate in thinking as weird as you can.

There is another pegging method for numbers known as **'Number Shape Method'**.

NUMBER SHAPE METHOD

In this method, instead of a rhyming word, we will associate an image with each number according to its shape which will remind us of that number.

Look at this table:

1 ONE	CANDLE	**2** TWO	DUCK
3 THREE	HEART	**4** FOUR	CHAIR
5 FIVE	HOOK	**6** SIX	HOCKEY STICK
7 SEVEN	AXE	**8** EIGHT	SNOW MAN

9 NINE	BALLOON	10 TEN	BAT BALL

In the given chart, you can see that we have associated each number with a shape that reminds us of that number. For instance, candle reminds us of number 1. Number 2 is curved like the neck of a duck. Number 3 can be seen as the top of the heart and so on.

MEMORIZING NAME OF THE WORLD'S HIGHEST MOUNTAIN PEAKS

Let's use this method to learn 10 highest mountain peaks in the world in the decreasing order of their height:

	Picture of number	Name of mountain	PNN	Visualization
1	Candle	Mt. Everest	Eve+rest	You are taking **rest** on a big **candle** at the peak of Mt. Everest.
2	Duck	K2	Kitten	A *kitten* is crossing the river while sitting on a **duck**.

	Picture of number	Name of mountain	PNN	Visualization
3	Heart	Kangchenjunga	King +chain+ jungle	*King* took out his **heart**, tied it to a *chain*, and hid it in *jungle*.
4	Chair	Lhotse	Hot+Say	You sit on a **chair** that is very *hot* and *say* 'Oh'.
5	Hook	Makalu	Mac+aloo	You are trying to eat *Mc Aloo* tikki burger that is hanging on the **hook**.
6	Hockey stick	Cho Oyu	Chor+you	People are running after *you* carrying **hockey sticks** shouting *'chor'*.
7	Axe	Dhaulagiri	Dhol+Aag+ giri (drum)+ (fire)+ (fall)	As soon as you beat a *dhol* with a long **axe**, fire *(aag)* falls *(giri)* from the sky.
8	Snow man	Manaslu	Man+slow	A **snowman** is walking with another *man* very *slowly*.

	Picture of number	Name of mountain	PNN	Visualization
9	Balloon	Nanga parbat	Nag+parbat (snake)+ (mountain)	A huge **balloon** is tied to a **nag** and is flying over a **parbat**.
10	Bat Ball	Annapurna	Anna (Anna Hazare)	*Anna Hazare* is playing with **bat ball** on the stage

So you can see that if in our imagination we use the shapes associated with the numbers, we can easily remember any given information in a sequence.

You can recall the information from any given point. For example, if we ask you that 'Makalu' is at which number in the list, you can easily remember that the 'Mc aloo tikki burger' was hanging on a *hook* and hook symbolizes number 5 or if we ask you what is the name of fourth highest mountain peak then '4' reminds you of a *chair* that was very *hot* and it further reminds you of the mountain 'Lhotse'.

In the same way, you can remember the list of Prime Ministers, Presidents, or any other information you are required to remember by number or hierarchical positions.

APPLICATIONS OF THE PEG SYSTEM

The peg system can be used for the same things as other mnemonic systems, including:

➢ Memorizing lists up 20 items in and out of sequence
➢ Remembering the item's position on the list

➢ Memorizing speeches in points
➢ Remembering information when it is inconvenient to write it down
➢ Keeping track of repetitive activities such as laps of a track or swimming pool, or repetitions of scales when practicing a musical instrument.

CHAPTER AT A GLANCE

❖ A 'peg' is like a mental hook that can help in holding information in our mind.

❖ It helps us in visualizing numbers which are intangible and difficult to visualize.

❖ In this method we associate an image to numbers according to their sound or shape.

❖ Once we decide on the images we can memorize any information given in numerical form by replacing numbers with respective images.

❖ Methods to create pegs for numbers:

   ➢ **Number rhyme method:** In this, we represent numbers by images of things that rhyme with it. For example 1 with 'sun' and 2 with 'shoe'.

   ➢ **Number shape method:** In this method, instead of a rhyming word, we associate an image with each number according to its shape which will remind us of that number.

❖ The peg system can be used for the same things as other mnemonic systems like:

   ➢ Memorizing lists up 20 items in and out of sequence

   ➢ Remembering the item's position on the list

   ➢ Memorizing speeches in points

   ➢ Remembering information when it is inconvenient to write it down

   ➢ Keeping track of repetitive activities such as laps of a track or swimming pool, or repetitions of scales when practicing a musical instrument etc.

13

MEMORIZING NUMERICAL FACTS AND DATA

Numbers play a very important role in our everyday life. There is lot of information that comprises numbers in various combinations, like bank account numbers, passwords, product codes, addresses, anniversary dates, credit card numbers, insurance policy numbers, etc.

A common thought that comes to everybody's mind is 'Why do we need to memorize numbers? Nowadays we have smartphones on which we can store all the relevant data, so much so that we don't even have to remember phone numbers.' But won't you agree with me that numbers always fascinate us? What if you have to give a sales presentation in your office? Wouldn't you like to amaze everyone by remembering all the sales figures and statistics at the back of your hand instead of referring to the papers or notes again and again? When we talk about *students,* they need to memorize a lot of numerical data like history dates, values of constants, periodic table, formulae, etc.

In the previous chapter, we have talked about the *number peg system,* wherein we gave some images to numbers based on their sound (rhyme) and shape. To memorize longer numbers, we make use of *Advance peg system* or **Phonetic peg system**. It is one of the most important techniques in the field of mnemonics. Memory masters all over the world use this technique along with other techniques to create records.

PHONETIC PEG SYSTEM

We are now going to learn a new language for memorizing numbers. Generally, whenever we learn a new language, the first thing we learn is the alphabet of that language. Then we use the letters of that alphabet to form words, then phrases, and finally sentences. In this method also, we will assign each number a letter and using those letters, we will make words by which we can group many numbers in a few words.

How chunking or grouping of numbers will help?

Let's understand it with a small example. If I ask you to memorize the 20 digit number:

'738 4195 921 321 8421 734'

Are you comfortable doing it? Don't you think it's highly confusing and difficult to memorize?

Now try memorizing the phrase, '*Comfortable appointment with friend camera*'. I think you can easily do it. Although this phrase consists of 40 characters and the above number contains only 20, why does it seems easy to memorize the phrase?

The reason is simple. In the second case, letters are used to form words, which are then joined to create some meaningful phrase whereas numbers are abstract and intangible. So, if we can convert these numbers also into words, they can be memorized easily. This is what phonetic system does.

PHONETIC CODES

Phonetic means speech sounds of letters of alphabet. In this method, we give specific codes to the numerals 0 to 9 on the basis of their phonic sound:

NUMBER	CODE
1	t or d
2	n
3	m
4	r
5	L
6	j, ch, sh or g (as in sage)
7	k or ga (as in gun)
8	f or, v
9	p or b
0	s or z

Remember:

❖ The five vowels (a, e, i, o, u) and the soft constant sounds wa, ha, ya are not assigned to any number.

❖ With some of the numbers, there is more than one letter given, but the phonetic sound of these letters is the same in each case. The lips, tongue, and teeth are used in the same identical way to sound 'p' and 'b' or 'f' and 'v' or 's' and 'z' or 'j', 'sh' and 'ch'.

Following hints can help you to memorize the above codes:

1   Small 't' or 'd' has one down stroke.

2   Small 'n' requires two down strokes.

3   'm' requires three down strokes or the shape of m is similar to 3.

4   Four in the majority of languages ends with 'r'. In Hindi, it's *Char*, in Latin its *Quarter*, in Russian its *Shutter*, etc.

5 In Roman 'L' means 50, here small 'l' means 5.

6 The mirror image of 6 is like 'j'. It can also be represented by the sounds 'ch' or 'sh' or 'dg'.

7 Two inverted sevens can form a 'k'.

8 The shape of the small 'f' (in running handwriting) is like 8.

9 'p' is the mirror image of 9, while 'b' can be turned around to look like 9.

0 Sun is round as a zero and the first alphabet of 'Sun' is 's'. Similarly, the first letter in 'Zero' is 'z'.

You need to practice it well to emboss this in your brain. Remember, it took you days to master alphabets in your childhood, so spend a little time getting this number phonic system down your memory. With little practice and clues given to remember them, you can master them easily.

Exercise your brain by filling the blanks in the table given below. If you are unable to recall the corresponding number or sound, go back and review the hints given after the phonetic table above to associate the phonic sound with the numbers:

4 = _____	k = _____	t = _____	6 = _____
S = _____	8 = _____	5 = _____	r = _____
j = _____	n = _____	3 = _____	f = _____
ch = _____	1 = _____	b = _____	9 = _____
m = _____	2 = _____	7 = _____	d = _____
L = _____	0 = _____	s = _____	p = _____

CREATING WORDS FROM NUMBERS

Now, using the above codes, we can translate any number into letters and can form a word which can be converted into an image for visualization.

Example 1:

    32

    3 = m   2 = n

    32 = m + n

Just think of some word that has the sound of 'm' and 'n' in it.

32 = m + n = moon

'MooN' is one of the possible words, you may think of some other words also like 'MaN', 'MeaN', MeNu, etc.

> *TIP:* While converting numbers into words, we may **add any vowel** (a, e, i, o, u) or any other letters in between the fixed codes that does not represent any number in the above phonetic codes table.
>
> When two or more words come to your mind for a particular number, choose the word you can see clearly in your mind.

Example 2:

    94

    9 = p or b   4 = r

As 9 has two letters according to the phonetic system, we just use any one of them and convert it into some word accordingly.

    94 = b + r

    94 = BeaR

Some other possible words: BaR, BoRe, BeeR, ,BooR

    94 = p + r

Some possible words: PeaR, PuRe, PuRi, PooR

Example 3:

994

994 = p + p + r

994 = **PaPeR** or it can be **PiPeR, PePpeR** also.

Using 9 as b, other possible words can be BieBeR.

Using the above method, you can convert any number into words or images.

HOW DOES PHONETIC SYSTEM HELP TO AVOID CONFUSION?

MEMORIZING AN ADDRESS

Suppose your friend invites you to his new residence. His house number is 124.

You might get confused whether it is 124 or 142. Now register this in your mind with the help of phonetic method.

1 2 4 = d n r

You can form a word '**donor**' from the letters 'd n r'

Visualization:

Imagine that your friend is a great donor and when you reach his house, he is donating all his belongings to his neighbours.

You can forget 124, but cannot forget your friend as a donor. Whenever word 'donor' will be converted into numbers, it will always be converted to 124; it can never give 142 or any other number.

MEMORIZING A LOCK CODE

Let's say you want to set a code to lock your suitcase and the code you set is 847.

It may be confusing for you to remember later whether it is 847 or 874 or 487. You can't afford to forget this; otherwise you won't be able to unlock your suitcase.

To remember this, convert 847 into an image by phonetic method.

8 4 7 = f r k

On seeing the letters frk, the word 'frock' comes immediately into mind.

Now you can visualize that there is a beautiful frock in your suitcase.

Had the lock code been 874, then corresponding 'fkr' can be thought as the word 'fakir'

You can get confused between numbers 847 and 874, but cannot confused between frock or fakir.

Thus phonetic peg system is very effective in memorizing numerical information correctly.

Here is a chart of some possible codes from 00 to 99 numbers, using phonetic pegs:

00	SauSe	01	SuiT	02	SuN	03	SuMo (wrestler)
04	SiR (Teacher)	05	SaLe	06	SaGe	07	Sky
08	SoFa	09	SoaP	10	DoSa	11	DaD
12	DeN	13	DaM	14	DR. (Doctor)	15	DoL (Doll)
16	DiSH	17	DecK	18	DwarF	19	TaP
20	NoSe	21	NeT	22	NuN	23	NeeM
24	NehRu (Jawaharlal Nehru)	25	NaiL	26	NaCHo (snack)	27	NecK
28	NiFe (knife)	29	NiPpo	30	MesS	31	MaT
32	MooN	33	MaM	34	aMiR	35	MaiL

36	MatCH (Stick)	37	MiKe	38	M.F. (Hussain)	39	MaP
40	RoSe	41	RaT	42	RaiN	43	RaM
44	ReaR	45	RaiL	46	RaJa (king)	47	RacK
48	RooF	49	RoPe	50	LaSe	51	LuDo
52	LioN	53	LiMe	54	LaRa (Brian)	55	LiLy
56	LeeCH	57	LaKe	58	LeaF	59	LaB
60	JuiSe	61	JeT	62	JeaN(s)	63	JaM
64	JaR	65	JaiL	66	JudGe	67	JacKy (Chan)
68	JeFe (boss)	69	JeeP	70	KisS	71	KiTe
72	KoNe (cone)	73	KoMb (comb)	74	KaR (Car)	75	KoaL (coal)
76	KaSH (Cash)	77	KaKe (Cake)	78	KoFee (Coffee)	79	KaP (Cap)
80	FuSe	81	FeeT	82	FaN	83	F.M. (Radio)
84	FiRe	85	FiLe	86	FiSH	87	FoK (fork)
88	FiFa	89	F.P. (Fountain Pen)	90	BuS	91	BaT

92	BuN	93	BoM (bomb)	94	BeaR	95	BelL
96	BuSH	97	BiKe	98	B.F (Best Friend)	99	Baby

These are the codes given for your reference; you can also make your own codes according to your choice following the rules given above for making the words from numbers.

SOUND IS MORE IMPORTANT THAN THE SPELLING

In the phonetic peg system, pay attention only to the sound or pronunciation of word and not to the spelling.

1. In case of Cone, Coal etc., the sound of *C* is like **K**, so we shall consider it like K, i.e. **coal** will be converted to **75** (koal).

2. **'Doll'** will not be converted into 155 but into **'15'** as we hear only one 'L', so we shall consider only one 'L' instead of two.

3. In **'Knife'**, we shall not consider 'k' since it is silent. Similarly, in **'Fork'** we shall not consider 'r' as it is silent. So, 'fork' will be **'87'**, and not 847.

4. The word **'accent'** will be pronounced as *'aksent'*. So, the letters *k, s, n, t* would correspond to number **7021** and not to 7721.

5. **'Sage'** will be converted to **06** not to 07 as in pronunciation of sage, g has a sound of 'j', which represents 6. But in words like kangaroo, g has a soft sound of 'ga' which represents '7' in phonetic language.

You might be thinking that it is very difficult to convert the numbers into such codes, but from our experience of teaching thousands of students in our workshops, we can assure you that once you are comfortable with the sounds of the numbers, the rest can be learnt in a matter of 2 days. To set in the sounds of the numbers in your memory, you have to start practicing from this very moment onwards.

Initially, you will find easier to transpose a word to a number as compared to transposing a number to a word since a word will be converted into a particular number only. But when a number is converted into a word, there are possibilities of forming more than one word, which can be a bit confusing in the beginning. The best way to overcome this is to master the words-to-numbers conversion first. Once you are comfortable with that, the number to word transposition will also become easy.

You will be able to use this system in your daily life more efficiently only if all these codes are on your figure tips.

MAKE IT A ROUTINE

Many people carry their daily newspaper along with them to office and as soon as they get time, they try to solve the crossword puzzle. You too can make it a habit of playing this mental game of transposing the words to numbers and numbers into words.

Example 4:
You might see the word '**beautiful**' written somewhere.
Break it down into numbers as '**9185**'
and the word '**letter**' would break down to '**514**'
(the double tt is the same sound as the single t here, thus representing 1 and not 11).
Whenever you see a number, think of its sound in your mind.

Example 5:
If you see a number **4285** on a number plate,
you should be able to read it as r,n,f,l,
which can further be converted into a word '**rainfall**'.

4285 = RaiNFalL
Now practice it by completing the following table:

Camera = _____	357 = _____
Comfortable = _____	140 = _____
Appointment = _____	914 = _____
Friend = _____	674 = _____
Monkey = _____	857 = _____
Shirt = _____	2394 = _____

* Refer to end of chapter for answers

MEMORIZING PHONE NUMBERS

Being too dependent on technology has its disadvantages. What would you do if, one day, you forget your phone at home and then get into trouble somewhere. Won't you feel helpless if you don't remember anybody's mobile number? You can use the Phonetic Peg system to memorize important mobile numbers with ease.

Let's say you want to memorize the mobile number of your aunt, i.e. **9810120337**

The first step is to divide the number in a group of two digits:
98/10/12/03/37

Now give phonetic codes to each group:
best friend dosa den sumo mike

Now, associate these words using the chain method:

Visualize that your aunt is sitting with her **best friend**, and both are eating a ***dosa*** in a ***dens***. Suddenly a ***sumo (wrestler)*** came, and your aunt starts screaming on a ***mike***.

This way you can memorize as many mobile numbers as you want.

RELATE AND IMAGINE

Caution: While visualizing the mobile number converted into words, always imagine the person whose number you are memorizing. This way there will be no confusion as to whose number it is.

MEMORIZING ATM PIN

Create one word for the four digit number (if possible) or create two images by dividing the number into two groups of two digits each.

    Bank ATM PIN number – **9421**

    9421 = p+ r + n + t

    9421 = **PRINT**

Visualization: Just imagine that as you insert your bank card in the ATM, the machines starts *printing* your account statement.

The same method can be applied to remember the codes of your locks for baggage, door, or lockers.

MEMORIZING 20-DIGIT NUMBERS AND BEYOND

Let's memorize the 20-digit number given at the beginning of this chapter, i.e.

    73841959213218421734

Write the letters corresponding to the given digits in the number below them:

    7384195921321 8421 734

    k m f r t b l p n t m n t f r n d k m r

Split these letters into small groups to form some words out of them:

    7384195921321 8421 734

    k m f r t b l p n t m n t f r n d k m r

Comfortable appointment friend camera (by adding vowels in between the characters)

So now it becomes easy to remember just four words or you can add a few more words to make more meaningful sentence like 'It is very **comfortable** to take an **appointment** with my **friend** to see his **camera**'.

> You may also split the numbers in group of two digits and use the phonetic codes memorized *(from 00 to 99)* to convert them into words and then visualize them using chain method.

Try it now:

73 = __KomB__

84 = _____

19 = _____

59 = _____

21 = _____

32 = _____

18 = _____

42 = _____

17 = _____

34 = _____

Now after converting these numbers into phonetic codes (which are images), memorize them by using the chain method *(refer to chapter 4)* or hide-and-seek method *(refer to chapter 9)*.

MEMORIZING BIRTHDATES AND ANNIVERSARIES

'Does your husband forget your birthday?'
'Never. I remind him of it in January and again in June,
and I always get two gifts in a year.'

Though the above anecdote is the exaggeration of the situation, many a times we do forget birthdays and anniversaries of important people in our life. Many a times we remember the month but get confused about the date. A friend of mine always wishes me one or two days before or after my birthday, as she always fails to remember the exact date.

Using memory techniques you can now remember them easily without any confusion.

Birthday or anniversary dates can be divided into two parts:

Numerical Part (date) + Month

Suppose you want to remember that your friend's birthday is on *23rd February*.

23	February
Numerical Part	*Month*

The numerical part can be converted into images by using the phonetic peg method. The 12 months can be given images according to some important day, event, or occasion occurring in that month.

Here are some such images for months:

MONTHS	IMPORTANT EVENT/ DAY	IMAGES
January	Beginning of a New Year	New Year Party
February	Valentine's Day	Rose

MONTHS	IMPORTANT EVENT/ DAY	IMAGES
March	Holi Festival	People playing with colours
April	April Fool's Day	Joker
May	Labour's Day	Labour working in some construction area
June	Summer Vacation	Holiday on Beach
July	Raining Season	Umbrella
August	Independence Day	National Flag
September	Teacher's Day	Teacher
October	Gandhi Jayanti	Gandhi Ji
November	Children's Day	Children playing in the classroom
December	Christmas	Santa Claus

If a particular month reminds you of some other important event from your life, you can relate its image accordingly.

Now your friend's **birthday** is on **23rd February**:

23: Neem *(phonetic code)*

February: Rose *(Valentine's day)*

Visualization:

Visualize that on her birthday, your friend is *cutting a cake* made up of **roses** and wearing a hat with **neem** leaves all over it.

Let's say your Boss' **anniversary** is on **2nd December**.

02: Sun *(phonetic code)*

December: Santa Claus

Visualization:

Visualize that your Boss is giving anniversary party on the **Sun** and **Santa Claus** is giving gifts to everybody.

Once you master this system of pegging, you will overcome a lot of hurdles related to memorizing day-to-day things.

LESSEN THE STUDENT'S BURDEN

We will see more usage of phonetic peg system in the **student's section** for learning the values of: *Cube, cube roots, square, square roots, reciprocals, history dates, constants, periodic table, number system, formulae, melting point, boiling point, etc.*

---

* ANSWERS:

Camera	= 734		357	= milk
Comfortable	= 384195		140	= tyres
Appointment	= 921321		914	= potter (harry)
Friend	= 8421		674	= joker
Monkey	= 327		857	= flock
Shirt	= 641		2394	= number

❖ To memorize long numbers, we use the Advanced Peg system or the Phonetic Peg system.

❖ In this method we assign a letter to numbers from 0–9 and using those letters we convert a group of numbers into meaningful words.

❖ Steps to memorize long numbers:

1. **Assign a phonetic code to each numeral**

NUMBER	CODE
1	t or d
2	n
3	m
4	r
5	L
6	j, ch, sh or g (as in sage)
7	k or ga (as in gun)
8	f or, v
9	p or b
0	s or z

The five vowels (a, e, i, o, u) and the soft constants sounds wa, ha, ya are not assigned to any number.

2. **Form meaningful words using those letters**

❖ While converting numbers into words, we may **add any vowel** (a, e, i, o, u) or any other alphabets in between the fixed codes.

Example: 94 = b + r ; 94= BeaRorBeeR

❖ When two or more words come to your mind for a particular number, choose that word which you can see clearly in your mind.

❖ Pay attention only to the sound or pronunciation of the word and not to the spelling.

3. **Use the chain method or the hide-and-seek method to memorize the sequence of words.**

❖ This technique can be used to memorize:

> ❯ Mobile numbers
> ❯ ATM pins
> ❯ Bank account numbers
> ❯ 20 digit numbers and beyond.
> ❯ Birthdays and anniversaries etc.

❖ In academics it can be used to memorize cube, cube roots, square, square roots, reciprocals, history dates, constants, periodic table, number system, formulae, melting point, boiling point, etc.

❖ Memory masters all over the world use this technique, along with other techniques, to create records.

14

CREATE YOUR OWN PEG SYSTEM

In the earlier chapters, we have repeatedly mentioned that the best way to remember things is through your own associations. You can follow whichever method you like or feel suitable but when you connect information on your own, it will stay with you for a longer period of time.

In the Peg system, you can form your own pegs for each number.

VALUE PEG SYSTEM

Like in the earlier chapters, we have associated numbers according to their rhyming sound or shapes. In the same way, numbers can be associated with something of the same value too. For example, number '1' can be given an image of a 'King' as there can only be one king in a kingdom. Or number '2' can be linked with 'eyes' or 'ears'. So, you can associate a particular number with something of the same value but the value of that should remain fixed. For example, you cannot link number '4' with four Sundays in a month because it is not fixed. There may be a month where there are five Sundays.

NUMBER	VALUE IMAGE
1	King
2	Eyes or Ears
3	Traffic Light
4	Car (4 wheels)
5	Glove (5 fingers)
6	Spider (6 legs)
7	Rainbow
8	Octopus (8 arms)
9	9 Hindu goddesses (9 Devis)
10	Ravan (10 heads) or total number of players in a basketball team

This method can also be called as 'Value Peg System' or 'Quantifying Method'.

ALPHABET PEG SYSTEM

The alphabet peg system works similar to the number peg system, the only difference being that instead of numbers, letters of alphabet are given images to be associated with the required information or data to be memorized.

While learning *ABC* in our childhood, we all learnt almost the same words starting with each letter. For example, almost everybody will have the same answer when asked 'A' for…?

The answer is: *Apple*.

So we will use the information that is etched in our mind for years as a link to memorize new information.

Another method is to associate the letter with a similar sounding word. Like **A** can be associated with *Hay* or *Way*, **B** can be imagined as a *Bee*, etc.

The following table presents two set of image words that can be used for the Alphabet Peg System. The first set of image words represent items that **start** with the corresponding letter and the second set represent items that **rhyme** with corresponding letter.

Letter	First letter	Rhyming Word
A	Apple	Hay
B	Boy	Bee
C	Cat	See or sea
D	Dog	Deep
E	Elephant	Eve/eel
F	Fan	Half

Letter	First letter	Rhyming Word
G	Goat	Jeans
H	Hut	Age
I	Ink	Eye
J	Jug	Jay (a type of bird)
K	Kite	Key
L	Lion	Elbow
M	Mango	Empty
N	Nest	Hen
O	Orange	Oh! Om
P	Parrot	Pea
Q	Queen	Queue
R	Rabbit	Oar
S	Ship	Ass
T	Toy	Tea
U	Umbrella	Huge
V	Van	Veil
W	Watch	Double you
X	X ray	Axe
Y	Yatch	Wire
Z	Zoo	Zebra

Application of Alphabet and Value Peg System is the same as the Rhyme and Shape Number Peg System.

MEMORIZING LIST OF PRIME MINISTERS

Using the alphabet peg system, try to memorize the list of Prime Ministers of India in a sequence. The first two associations are given for you; you can try to memorize the rest using your imagination:

S. No.	Prime Minister	PNN for Names	Alphabet Pegs	Visualization
1.	Jawahar Lal Nehru	Chacha Nehru	Apple	Chacha Nehru is eating an apple
2.	Gulzari Lal Nanda	Golzari in lal (red)	Boy	Boy is wearing clothes made up of golzari in lal (red) colour
3.	Lal Bahadur Shastri	Bahadur	Cat	
4.	Indira Gandhi		Dog	
5.	Morarji Desai		Elephant	
6.	Chowdhary Charan Singh		Fan	
7.	Rajiv Gandhi		Goat	
8.	V.P. Singh		Hut	

S. No.	Prime Minister	PNN for Names	Alphabet Pegs	Visualization
9.	Chandra Shekhar		Ink	
10.	P.V. Narsimha Rao		Jug	
11.	Atal Bihari Vajpayee		Kite	
12.	H.D. Deve Gowda		Lion	
13.	I.K. Gujral		Mango	
14.	Atal Bihari Vajpayee		Nest	
15.	Dr Manmohan Singh		Orange	
16.	Narendra Modi		Parrot	

CHAPTER AT A GLANCE

❖ We can associate the numbers with images according to their value as well. This method can also be called 'Value Peg System' or 'Quantifying Method'.

❖ For example, number 1 can be associated with King and number 2 can be associated with eyes or ears and so on.

❖ In the **Alphabet Pegging System** we assign images to letters of the English alphabet instead of numbers.

❖ The images can be given on the basis of the sound of the letter or the words which begin with the letter.

❖ Application of **Value Peg System** or **Alphabet Peg System** is the same as the Number Peg System.

1 5

MIND MAPS—CREATIVE NOTE TAKING

Now it is clear that having a good memory is not an innate human capability. Rather it is a skill that can be acquired and improved over time. The important thing is that it must be practiced like any other mental skill. In the previous chapters, we have learnt various methods of improving one's memory through the principles of association and imagination.

Think of a HORSE. What is the first thing that comes to your mind? The spelling 'H', 'O', 'R', 'S', 'E' or a picture of the horse?

It most certainly will be the second. The reason this happens so naturally is because the brain 'stores' information more easily in the form of **pictures**.

Two components of improving memory have already been introduced to you: association and imagination. The third important component is representing the information *pictorially*. Indeed a picture is worth a thousand words. This is more so with respect to storing the information and recalling it with ease. Mind Map is one such tool that helps integrate these two very important aspects of the brain's functioning: association and pictorial representation.

In this chapter, we are going to introduce you to **MIND MAP®**, which will not only help you improve your memory but also help you to be organized in your work. The act of Mind Mapping increases association, imagination, and creativity—**so it is the perfect tool to improve memory.**

WHAT IS A MIND MAP?

Mind map is a creative and effective means of note taking invented by author and educational consultant *Tony Buzan*.

Mind map is a graphical technique whichoffers an overview of a topic and complex information in a visual form, where we start with a **central idea** and expand outward to morein-depth subtopics on **branches**. Each branch holds a key image or **key word** printed on the line. Details are added to the main branches and radiate out.

Its structure is more of a radial type, like that of a tree seen from the top branching out in all directions from the trunk. Or it can be compared to a city map, where different main roads starting from a central point of a city radiatein all directions, further branching into sub roads and lanes spreading throughout the city like a web till the outskirts of the city.

Mind maps have many applications in *personal, family, educational, and business situations,* including:

- ✤ taking notes during a lecture or a business meeting,
- ✤ summarizing a topic or a chapter you are studying for your exams,
- ✤ making notes while reading,
- ✤ mapping out your thoughts while planning an event,
- ✤ setting career goals
- ✤ brainstorming various possibilities to work out a problem

But before going in to the details of its usage, first let's learn how to create a mind map.

HOW TO MAKE MIND MAPS?

To draw a mind map, do the following:

1. Turn your page on its side *(landscape)*, making sure that it is a blank paper.
2. **Start at the centre with an image** of the main subject (or main idea) using at least 3 colours (image speaks a thousand words). Starting in the centre gives your brain freedom to spread out in all directions and to express yourself more freely and naturally.
3. **Add the main branches** representing the subject's main topics or themes using **key words and images.**
4. **Add sub-branches** to the main branches, having further detail with more key words and images.
5. Make your **branches curved** rather than straight-lined.
6. Use **colours** throughout and make your Mind Map as beautiful as possible.
7. Write your **words clearly in print** and use only **one word per line.**
8. **Use arrows to connect linking ideas.** Your brain works by association. It likes to link two or three things together. Linking the branches will help you make connections and understand and remember a lot more easily.

WHY MIND MAPS?

Mind maps can be more effective than other brainstorming and linear note-taking methods for a number of reasons:

❖ A mind map can at once give you an overview of a large subject while also holding large amounts of information on a single page.

❖ Instead of boring, linear note making, the combinations of words and images with colours makes it more memorable and enjoyable to create and review.

❖ It combines both left and right brain thinking, which means that you will remember the information better than if you just had lines of words.

❖ It mimics the way our brains think—bouncing ideas off each other.

❖ You can generate ideas very quickly with this technique and are encouraged to explore different creative pathways.

In one survey, executives who started using mind mapping said they were able to work significantly faster than before and juggle more complex projects through mind mapping. And research suggests **mind mapping can improve learning and memory by 10 to 15 percent** versus conventional note-taking and studying techniques.

The whole concept of mind maps, what they are, why to use them, how mind maps can be made and their uses all have been summarized in the following mind map:

Mind Map about the concept of Mind Mapping

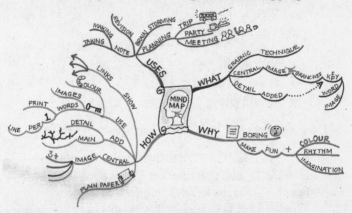

see appendix II 'mind maps' for colourful image of the above mind map

MIND MAP ABOUT PLANNING A PARTY

Planning may be done for organizing a farewell party or a trip to the US or planning your schedule for the coming weekend.

Let's say you have to plan your son's birthday party. A little planning goes a long way towards making things run more smoothly and in an organized way without any last minute hassles.

Mind mapping helps you plan ahead by seeing the whole picture with all the good and bad possibilities. Here is a mind map presenting some of the possibilities and options. You can map out your own perfect party.

Step-by-step mind mapping your party:

1. First of all, draw a central image on a blank page, turned sideways, presenting your party. You can make it catchy by drawing a cake or a balloon on it.
2. Draw your big main branches coming off this image. These branches may give you answers to the following:
    - ❖ When to have a party?
    - ❖ Where to have it?
    - ❖ Who will be invited?
    - ❖ Theme of the party
    - ❖ Food
    - ❖ Music
    - ❖ Games
    - ❖ Return gifts

Draw each branch in a different colour to make it stand out.

3. Once you have the main branches, you can add sub-branches by adding further details and options to the main branch. For example, while thinking of where to have the party, you can have options like whether to have it at home or a nearby club or a restaurant. Draw a different branch for each of your options.

4. You can keep on adding extra branches and putting in as much detail as you like. You will be amazed by the number of ideas coming out of your mind that otherwise you might not have thought had you not been using a mind map.

After looking at all the possibilities, you can choose the best options according to your time, budget, and comfort. You can further plan what work you will do and what work you will delegate to your spouse or friend etc.

Similarly, mind maps can be used to give presentations, brainstorming the possibilities of increasing the productivity or efficiency of the company, summarizing the points of meeting, etc.

Mind Map about planning a birthday party

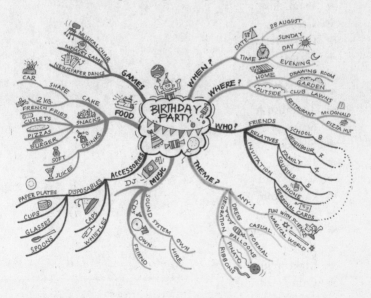

see appendix II 'mind maps' for colourful image of the above mind map

MIND MAP ABOUT PLANNING A TRIP

Usually, when we have to go for a trip, we make a list of all the things, to be carried and check with it while packing our luggage. Let's say I have to for a trip to US for some workshop. Below is the list of items given that I need to pack:

- Visa
- Passport
- Books
- Pen drive
- Suits
- Towel
- Band-aids
- Cash
- Organizer address
- Tickets
- Shawl
- Gifts
- Toothbrush
- Soaps
- Snacks
- Laddoo
- Credit card
- Cold cream
- Thyronorm
- Friends address
- Laptop
- Makeup kit
- Other medicines

Now every time I pack something in the suitcase, I put a tick on it and then search what is left in this random list, which is time consuming.

Instead of this, if I could convert it into a mind map as shown below, then things would be very easy. While making the mind map, I have divided the items of the whole list under different categories (branches) marked by different colours, making each category unique and distinct. Now if I have to check about what medicines I have left, I just need to go to that branch and check. Likewise, it helps me to further add on some items which I might have missed to write.

So a mind map not only helps to check the list, it also helps in creating the list.

Mind Map about planning a US Trip

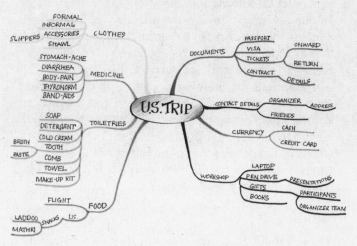

see appendix II 'mind maps' for colourful image of the above mind map

MIND MAP ABOUT MAKING NOTES OF A TOPIC

To understand the importance of a mind maps in summarizing a topic, let's take an example:

Read the following passage of **200 words**:

'Mahatma Gandhi, one of the greatest leaders of India, had his own views on English education. He held the view that **colonial education** would create a **sense of inferiority in** the **minds of Indians**. It would make them think that **Western civilization** was **superior** to Indian civilization and destroy the pride that they had in their culture. Education in English would cripple Indians; **distance** them **from** their **own social surroundings**. According to him, Western education focused on reading and writing rather than on oral knowledge; it **valued textbooks rather than** lived experience and **practical knowledge.** He strongly felt that **Indian languages** ought to be the medium of instruction because this would make **easier** for them **to understand** the whole thing and would enable them to **recover** their sense of **dignity** and **self-respect.** Mahatma Gandhi laid **emphasis** on **learning** a **craft** as it would make them work with their own hands and get a **practical knowledge** of the whole thing. By doing so they would learn how different things are operated. The learning of a craft would develop not only their mind but also their capacity to understand. Later on such a thing could **help** many **to earn** their own living'.

You will realize that a few words in the above passage are in bold. These are the **keywords** that **summarize** the whole passage **in just 20 percent (39 words)** of the total word count.

The rest 80 percent (161 words) are non key words or connectors that are not required while revising the passage. If you revise only keywords, you get all the required information and it saves lot of your time as you have to read only around 20 percent of the total passage.

Let's see how you can visualize this paragraph in the form of a mind map, using these keywords and relevant images:

Mind Map about views of Gandhi ji on English education

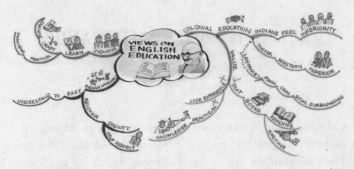

see appendix II 'mind maps' for colourful image of the above mind map

Just by designing a mind map you will be able to recall the complete information in a few minutes. As mentioned earlier, our mind recalls images faster than the text, especially, an image that you have designed yourself.

HOW DO MIND MAPS IMPROVE MEMORY?

The act of mind mapping increases association, imagination, and creativity—so it is the perfect tool to improve memory.

So how exactly do mind maps improve memory? Let's take a look:

- Mind maps only contain keywords. This means that the information to remember is prompted by short, memorable words with meaning.
- Mind maps promote associations and connections. As we know, association is an important way to improve memory.
- Mind maps use colours and images that stimulate your imagination. Imagination is the key secret to improve memory.

16

HOW TO IMPROVE CONCENTRATION

Concentration is the process of taking your mind off many random thoughts and putting it on one thought/task at a time. The success of the task at hand depends mainly on the level of concentration or concentrated efforts put in it.

Sunlight seems pleasant to all and is necessary for our existence. But not everyone is aware that when the same pleasant sunrays are passed through a convex lens and made to fall on a piece of paper, they can burn the paper. *How did the rays acquire this power?* It was the result of making them converge and thereby, 'concentrated' at one point.

Our mind works on the same principle. **When it is focused on a thought or an activity, like a sharp ray of the sun, we can achieve unbelievable results.**

Our mind is always occupied with various thoughts. However, to concentrate on a particular task, it is necessary that our mind should not wander. It should remain bound to essential thoughts only. To increase concentration and achieve such a state of mind, the following 7measures are recommended:

1. Concentration exercises
2. Observation skills
3. Food for brain
4. Keeping a check on your lifestyle
5. Avoiding multi-tasking
6. Setting clear goals
7. Forgetting unwanted memories
8. Meditation

CONCENTRATION EXERCISES

1. **Do something different everyday**—To develop flexibility and adaptability to change in your life, you must do something different everyday like:

   ❖ Shop at a different store.
   ❖ Take a different route home.
   ❖ Read a book on an unfamiliar subject.
   ❖ Try out new recipes.
   ❖ Try thinking 10 innovate uses of a pen or any other object.
   ❖ Close your eyes and sense your way slowly around a room.
   ❖ Involve yourself in a new game or sport, like bowling, karate, roller-skating etc.

The sameness of everyday routine is a death knell for your brain. For complete usage of your brain, diverse stimulation is the key. It also gets you unstuck from habits and ruts that are brining you unfavourable results.

2. **Use your body in new ways**—Switch your handedness and comb your hair, brush your teeth, stir your coffee, or do other simple tasks with your **non-dominant hand**.

3. **Spell words backwards**—This is great for kids as well and has the added bonus of helping them to spell.

4. **Count common words in a paragraph.** Count words like 'it' or 'and' without using a finger to point to it.

5. **Doing simple mathematical calculations** in your head is a very good exercise to improve concentration.

6. **Recalling the objects**—Look in your refrigerator briefly, but thoroughly. Then close the door and enumerate the items contained therein. Do the same with the room of your house, a display window in a shop, or a detailed picture on a wall.

7. **Review your thoughts**—At the end of every hour, review what happened to you during the previous 60 minutes. This is a good practice for being mindful throughout the day, and should only take a few seconds. At the day's end, mentally review all the events that happened to you throughout the day up to your present point. Memory gaps about your day's events reveal unconscious moments.

8. **Do crosswords and puzzles**—Practice doing crosswords and word jumbles daily.

9. **Play board games**—Playing board games like Scrabble, Chinese Checkers, and especially Chess are very good for exercising the brain. Any game that requires you to use Math and language skills are tapping into those areas of your brain that may need some stirring.

10. **Read riddle books** and try to solve them. These also make good party icebreakers.

Some brainteasers and puzzles for practice:

1. MATCHSTICK PUZZLES:

(i)   Change 3 matches to create 3 squares:

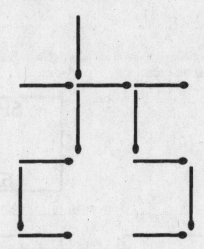

(ii)   Change 2 matches to create 4 squares

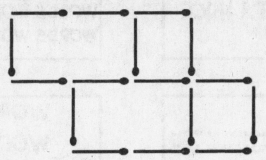

2. LOOK AT THE FOLLOWING IMAGES AND TRY TO WORK OUT THEIR FULL MEANING...

N
 I
  A
   G
    A
     R
      A

AGED
AGED ←
AGED

a.   *Niagara Falls*   b. _____

HIGH HIGH

SHUT

SIT

c. _____   d. _____

STA4NCE

FUNNY FUNNY
WORDS WORDS
WORDS WORDS

e. _____   f. _____

PERSONALITY

g. _____   h. _____

See the answers at the end of the chapter.

OBSERVATION SKILLS

One of the secrets to good memory is **observation.** To be able to observe better, you need to be attentive and focused. If you are not attentive, you can't be observant and if you are not observant, you can't have a good memory.

All of us wear watches. Without looking at your watch, recall whether at the 12 o' clock position, your watch has digits, roman numbers, or simply dots. Can you recall what it is? Now quickly look at your watch. Were you correct? No? You look at your watch so many times a day but still can't say for sure. The reason is that although we see the watch many a times, we don't observe it.

We cannot remember anything if do not observe it carefully. It is the eyes that see. But it is the brain that interprets. Observation is really a matter of habit. Observing people and situations is an incredibly valuable tool to improve your concentration. It gives you the ability to notice subtle cues during conversations, job interviews, presentations, and anywhere else so you can react to situations more tactfully.

Many people must have witnessed an apple falling to the ground just as Newton did. However, Newton observed the instance keenly and thought about it, unlike others, who saw but did not observe. It was only due to Newton's observation skills that he arrived at the laws of gravity.

Though there are a number of other ways to strengthen your observation, if you do not transfer these principles to your day-to-day functioning and make it a habit, there will be no lasting impact on the powers of concentration.

EXERCISES TO IMPROVE OBSERVATION AND
RECOLLECTION SKILLS

  1. Take a pen and a piece of paper and from your memory try to list out all the things from any one of the rooms in

your house—the furniture, pictures, showpieces, books, etc. without actually going inside the room. After listing the items, go back to the room and look at everything you missed, things you saw countless time but didn't observe. Now observe everything closely. Repeat the test and you will see that the list is now longer. Keep doing this everyday and you will get better at it. You can do this exercise with anything: people's faces, clothes, objects, dogs etc. Basically *anything with a lot of detail.*

2. Give yourself some simple observation tasks everyday. For instance, if you are going to parties, observe the clothes worn by 5 people. After returning home, try to recollect the details. You may increase the number to 10 after a few days of practice.

3. While shopping for food items, say biscuits, try and observe how many brands of biscuits are available, what are the colours of their packaging, the difference in their prices, the flavour, etc.

4. Observation tests are excellent tools to both improve and track your improvements.

   (i)   Read the sentence below:
         FINISHED FILES ARE THE
         RESULTS OF YEARS OF SCIENTIFIC
         STUDY COMBINED WITH THE
         EXPERIENCE OF YEARS

The question: How many times do you see the letter F in the sentence above? Count them only once!

   (ii) All of the items are unique to each picture, apart from one item. Find that item:

See the answers at the end of the chapter.

You may practice more such puzzles for finding differences in two similar images on the website:

http://www.spotthedifference.com/

**Observation is a skill that takes time to hone.
Keep practicing, even if you think you will never improve
your awareness.**

FOOD FOR BRAIN

Just like every organ in the body needs food for nourishment, the brain needs to be fed too. Though the brain is relatively a small organ, weighing about 1.4 kilo, about **2 percent of the total body weight,** it uses about **20 percent of the oxygen** that is used by the entire body while at rest and eats up about a quarter of the energy produced by the body. In fact the brain is the largest consumer of the energy that our body produces. Just like petrol fills your car, glucose fills your brain. In the absence of proper supply of glucose to the brain, the ability of the brain to concentrate is affected badly and leads to short-term memory loss and fatigue.

One more culprit that can often lead to some loss of memory over the years is the generation of **free radicals** in the body. Free radicals are the toxic forms of oxygen that are created during normal cellular reactions. Small amount of free radicals in the body are a good thing, but too much of their  bombardment accelerate ageing and diseases. Food containing more of antioxidants or antioxidant supplements can help to protect from the damage caused by free radicals excess.

Antioxidants can be vitamins, minerals, hormones, or enzymes. Although a certain amount is manufactured in the body as enzymes or hormones, most of the antioxidants come from fruits and vegetables.

So along with the constant supply of the glucose to the brain, it also needs good amount of antioxidants to take care of free radical damage.

Researchers have proved that certain kind of food play a significant role in the improvement of memory and keeping the brain cells active. Some of them are:

Whole grain cereals	❖ Release glucose to keep you alert ❖ Good source of zinc and vitamin B-complex group
Walnuts	❖ Rich in Vitamin E ❖ Reduce risk of Alzheimer's
Pumpkin seeds	❖ Source of omega 3 fatty acids ❖ Improve brain's performance

Tomatoes	❖ Contain an antioxidant called lycopene ❖ Prevent free radicals from damaging brain cells ❖ Enhance attention span, memory and problem-solving skills
Broccoli	❖ Great source of vitamin K ❖ Enhance cognitive function and improve brain power
Citrus and fresh fruits	❖ Rich in vitamin C which is an important antioxidant ❖ Keep the brain alert
Spinach	❖ Has high potassium levels ❖ Increases the speed of signals sent between neurons, making the brain more responsive
Blueberries	❖ Contains antioxidants including anthocyanins and proanthocyanidins ❖ Boost concentration, memory, and focus, ❖ Protect against cancer, heart disease, and dementia
Green tea	❖ Contains less caffeine as compared to tea or coffee ❖ Provide antioxidants and flavonoids ❖ Helps offset the effects of alcohol by repairing liver damage

Leafy green vegetables	❖ Full of antioxidants and carotenoids, B-vitamins and folic acid ❖ Boosts your brain power increases focus and mental clarity
Water	❖ Gives the brain the electrical energy for all brain functions, including thought and memory processes ❖ Helps you think faster, be more focused, and experience greater clarity and creativity
Herbs like Ginkgo, Ginseng, Brahmi and Amino acids like L-carnitine	❖ Prevents the degenerative conditions of the brain and other vital organs ❖ Improves overall cognitive functions and sharpen mental focus ❖ Increasing blood flow and consequently the supply of oxygen and nutrients to the brain ❖ Protect against cellular damage ❖ Very useful for the aged suffering from memory loss and senile dementia ❖ Improves memory and memory related functions by enhancing the efficiency of nerve impulse transmission

KEEPING A CHECK YOUR LIFESTYLE

Modern lifestyle has its drawbacks like poor diet, stress, lack of sleep, smoking, pollution etc. which damage fragile brain cells. Certain pharmaceutical drugs and alcohol also cause severe memory loss. The level of pollution of various kind leads to behavioural problem and learning difficulties in kids which persist in adulthood. Alzheimer's has become so common that it is now accepted as a disease of the elderly.

Some of the things that we need to check and change in our lifestyle are discussed in this section:

A: FOOD INTAKE

Some suggestions for the proper intake of food are:

1. AVOID JUNK FOOD

Today junk food has become a part of modern lifestyle. We all know that eating junk food on a regular basis is not only harmful for our brain cells but also for our overall health. So I am not going to advise you not to eat junk food, as you already know it quite well.

Instead I would like to ask you a simple question.

Do you think if we use the petrol we use in car to run an airplane, it will fly smoothly?

Isn't airplane fuel more refined?

Well, we can't use normal petrol in an airplane because we know that while driving a car if some impurity comes in the petrol, at the most, the car will stop on the road. We can leave the car on the road and tow it later or call a mechanic. But we can't take such a risk in the case of an airplane.

How do you want your life to be? Like an airplane flying high at a good speed without any brakes or like a car that can stop anywhere? Now the choice is yours. If you want to travel in a smooth safe flight, check the quality of petrol you are putting into your vehicle, i.e. the kind of food you are giving to your body.

Here are some shocking facts about junk food to help you decide its harmful effects on the body:

- ❖ 99 percent fast food contains a taste-enhancing agent called **MSG** *(Monosodium Glutamate),* which is responsible for more than 90 percent diseases in our body, including cancer, heart attack, high blood pressure, tooth decay, and other diseases.
- ❖ Fats from junk food trigger the urge to eat more. This effect can last for several days.
- ❖ *Aspartine*, an artificial low calorie sweetener, commonly included in most of the fast food and soft drinks, is approximately 200 times sweeter than sugar and causes a number of mental illnesses. Neuroscience says sometimes the symptoms appear only after 90 percent of the neurons of a particular area are dead.
- ❖ Heavy consumption of soft drinks spills out huge amount of calcium, magnesium, and other trace mineral from our body.
- ❖ To neutralize the ill effects of a glass of soft drink, the human body needs 32 glasses of water intake.

TAKING THE 'JUNK' OUT OF JUNK FOOD

Here are few tips on how you can include healthy food in your daily routine even while eating out.

- ❖ Choose fast-food restaurants that offer healthier choices.
- ❖ Opt for food and beverages that are made up mostly of ingredients that offer nutrients along with calories.
- ❖ Enjoy freshly squeezed orange juice instead of canned juices or soft drinks. Avoid other sweetened beverages.
- ❖ Buy a grilled sandwich or a whole-grain bun instead of chips with processed cheese sauce, frozen pizza rolls or French fries.

2. AVOID DRUGS

A number of prescriptions and over-the-counter medications can interfere with our memory. Antidepressants, anti-anxiety medicines, muscle relaxants, tranquilizers, sleeping pills, and pain medications given after surgery can have a negative impact on  our brain. As you age and your metabolism slows down, medicines tend to stay in the system for longer and this can also have an adverse effect on you.

Make a list of the medicines you are taking, including any purchased from your pharmacy, and take it to your doctor. They can decide if you have any drug-related memory problems and alter your medication if necessary. Also, avoid self-medication at any cost.

3. AVOID ALCOHOL

In today's stressful life, heading to a bar to take off that stress for a while or pouring yourself a glass of wine while socializing amongst your friends may seem tempting options. However, alcohol has proved to only make concentrating more difficult. You cannot drink and think (too well) at the same time.

4. ADOPTING A VEGETARIAN LIFESTYLE

In earlier times, a lot of studies supported non-vegetarian diet but now the pendulum has swung the other way. Latest researches show that a vegetarian diet helps to boost your memory and concentration. Earlier the studies focused on nutritional deficiencies of a vegetarian diet but now they confirm the health benefits of meat free diet. In July 2009, the American Dietetic Association weighed in with a position paper, concluding that 'appropriately planned vegetarian diets, including total vegetarian or vegan diets, are healthful, nutritionally adequate, and may provide health benefits in the prevention and treatment of certain diseases' (*Journal of the American Dietetic Association, July 2009*).

BENEFITS OF BEING VEGETARIAN

❖ **You'll ward off diseases:** An estimated 70 percent of all diseases, including one-third of all cancers, are diet related. A vegetarian diet reduces the risk for chronic degenerative diseases such as obesity, coronary artery disease, high blood pressure, diabetes and certain types of cancer including colon, breast, prostate, stomach, lung, and esophageal cancer. A vegetarian diet is inherently healthful because vegetarians consume less animal fat and cholesterol (vegans consume no animal fat or cholesterol) and instead consume more fibre and more antioxidant-rich produce. *Fibre-rich foods also help to prevent constipation.*

❖ **You'll live longer:** Studies show that you can add about 13 healthy years to your life by switching from a non-vegetarian diet to a vegetarian one. Residents of Okinawa, Japan, have the longest life expectancy among Japanese and most likely the longest life expectancy in the world, according to a 30-year study of more than 600 Okinawan centenarians. Their secret: a low-calorie diet of unrefined complex carbohydrates, fibre-rich fruits and vegetables, and soy.

❖ **You'll reduce your risk of food-borne illnesses:** Foods rich in protein such as meat, poultry, fish, and seafood are frequently involved in food-borne illness outbreaks.

❖ **You'll avoid toxic chemicals:** Fish, in particular, contain carcinogens (PCBs, DDT) and heavy metals (mercury, arsenic, lead, cadmium) that can't be removed through cooking or freezing. Meat can also be laced with steroids and hormones, harmful for the human body.

Names of some famous personalities who are vegetarian
Dr Abdul Kalam, Martina Naratilova, Albert Einstein,
Amitabh Bachchan, Morarji Desai, M.K. Gandhi, Anil
Kumble, Srinivasa Ramanujan, Sachin Tendulkar,
Rabindarnath Tagore, Leonardo Da Vinci, Abraham
Isaac Kook, Leo Tolstoy, Sir Edwin Arnold,
Chelsea Clinton

B: PHYSICAL EXERCISE

Exercise increases the flow of
oxygen-rich blood to the brain,
promoting clear thinking and
sharper recall. It helps to maintain
a healthy blood-sugar level and
also releases positive chemicals in
the brain, which can help stimulate
memory function. Regular exercise
helps us to cope with stress and to stay healthy, all of which lead to
better concentration and memory.

DID YOU KNOW???

It is a proven fact now that exercise helps brain to release
BDNF (Brain Derived Neurotrophic Factor). Whereas
neurotransmitters carry out signaling, neurotrophins
such as BDNF build and maintain the cell circuitry—
the infrastructure itself. Researchers found that if they
sprinkled BDNF onto neurons in a petri dish, the cells
automatically sprouted new branches, producing the
same structural growth required for learning, making
BDNF the fertilizer that encourages neurons to connect
to one another and grow, making it vital for neuroplasticity

and neurogenesis. Neuro Plasticity is the innate ability of the brain to transform/change in response to external and internal stimuli. Neuro Genesis is the phenomenon of new neurons taking birth inside the brain every single day. Both NeuroPlasticity and NeuroGenesis are required for learning and memory. Now there is a direct link between exercise and improvement in memory through the link of BDNF. John J. Ratey has written an excellent book called *SPARK*, which gives many more details about how Physical Exercise impacts Brain in a very positive way.

Even after knowing the benefits of physical exercise, we give less importance to it as we are busy with our work and gadgets. Even children now-a-days don't do enough physical activities as they spend most of their playing time on computers and mobile phones.

Once a wise man was asked, *'What do you think is the strangest thing about human beings?'* He replied, *'The strangest thing about human beings is that first they invest their health to gain wealth and later they reinvest their wealth to regain their health'*.

There are plenty of ways to make sure you are getting regular physical exercise:

- ✤ For short journeys, walk rather than taking the bus or car
- ✤ Use the stairs instead of the lift or escalator
- ✤ Join a fitness, dance or yoga class
- ✤ If you work in an office, go out for a walk at lunchtime rather than staying at your work desk
- ✤ Plan with friends to go jogging or play tennis, for example, on a regular basis

C: AVOID WATCHING TOO MUCH TV

Watching TV is something virtually everyone enjoys, but did you know that TV can actually be harmful for you? What you consider to be a harmless past time can pose a real threat to your physical and mental well-being.

Some of the ways in which watching too much television adversely affects your brain are mentioned below.

✤ **Television makes your brain dull**

You might find it unbelievable but the fact is that your brain is more active when you are sleeping than when you are watching television. Excessive television viewing can have a detrimental effect on the health of your brain as it is largely determined by how much you actively use your brain. It may also cause degenerative brain disorders later in life such as dementia and Alzheimer's disease.

One of the reasons why brain activity is low when watching television is you don't really have to do any thinking. When you read, for example, you have to mentally create images of what you are reading. So while doing so, you are effectively exercising your brain.

Infact, **reading** may help to offset some of the harmful effects television has on the brain.

✤ **Short attention span**

Excessive television viewing can cause a person to develop a short attention span and increase the risk of attention deficit hyperactivity disorder (ADHD) in children and adults. This is thought to be due to the frequent scene changes that occur with modern-day video edits.

If you compare an old film, such as the ones from 1950s or 1960s, with films of today for example, you will notice that older movies had much longer scene changes. Cuts that occur too frequently can make a video difficult to follow and may even make you feel giddy.

❖ **Impaired brain development in children**

Watching television appears to be especially harmful for children as their brain has not yet fully developed. Increased television viewing in children tends to impair frontal lobe development which is responsible for impulse control and one's ability to concentrate. This may result in in appropriate behavior and learning difficulties in school.

❖ **A perfect tool to program the mind**

The main concern with watching TV is that you have no control over the content that your mind is exposed to. Some things shown in various programmes may be good, while others may not be so. TV provides easy access to all kinds of things to your subconscious mind. Various programmes shown on different channels may create a feeling of inferiority, increases expectations, and can even instill fear in impressionable mind of young people. Programmes related to crime and violence also sometimes result in real life crime.

Children often imitate what they see on-screen. The negative effects of TV violence are being passed on to young children and that's one of the major reasons of **increasing aggression amongst children as well as youth. Although your mind knows that whatever is shown on TV is not real, your subconscious believes it to be real.**

❖ **Piling on extra kilos:** Most of the times when people eat while watching TV, they often end up eating more than required, especially if they are munching on their favourite snack like chips or biscuits or sweetened beverages and the result is those bulges around your back and waste. That's why in the 1990s man was flat while the TV was broad and in today's scenario, the TV has gone flat and the man ...!!

* **Addiction**: Watching TV causes the body to release chemicals called 'endorphins' that make the body feel good. These endorphins are a natural sedative with properties similar to heroin. It is therefore not only possible, but probable, to become physically addicted to TV. A person who is unable to view their favorite television programme is likely to display similar withdrawal symptoms as a drug addict. He may become angry, anxious, and will go to great lengths to watch his programme.

I am not saying don't watch TV at all. All you need to do is control the time you spend on it and also keep a check on the content you are watching. You can utilize your spare time inmore useful activities like exercise, reading, interacting with friends and family, and activities that are crucial for achievement of your personal goals.

D: GOOD SLEEP

It is no secret that a good night's sleep makes you feel better. It not only gives your body time to relax and recharge, it also crucial to your brain's ability to learn and remember. When you go to sleep, your brain is still awake. In fact,

when you sleep the consumption of oxygen to the brain increases because at that time your brain is busy in reorganizing all the information that got stored in it throughout the day and forming memories. In children and teens, sleep also helps support growth and development.

The key thing is to stick to a regular sleeping pattern so that your body can maintain a regular rhythm. Try to get up at the same time every day, even on weekends. Students and people who sleep and wake up at different times during the day often face problems of concentration. The same problem is faced by students who reduce their sleeping time during exam days.

AMOUNT OF SLEEP NEEDED

Everyone's individual sleep needs vary as each one of us have different routine, eating habits, work pattern etc. In general, most healthy adults are built for 16 hours of wakefulness and need an average of 8 hours of sleep a night. Contrary to common myth, the need for sleep doesn't decline with age, but the ability to sleep for 6–8 hours at one time may be reduced.

Younger people seem to need more sleep than older people and the former (particularly babies, who sleep for about 12 hours a day) have more information to lay down into memories.

HOW TO GET A GOOD NIGHT'S SLEEP

Sleep problems are usually caused by lifestyle rather than a sleep disorder. If you are sleep deprived, you are at a risk of developing a number of serious health problems and your ability to learn and retain new information may be impaired. Sleep is essential for effective memory storage and retrieval.

According to leading sleep researchers, there are techniques to combat common sleep problems:

- ❖ Keep a regular sleep/wake schedule
- ❖ Comfortable pillows and mattresses are also important

- ❖ Don't drink or eat caffeine 2–3 hours before bed and minimize daytime use
- ❖ Don't smoke, especially near bedtime or if you get up in the night
- ❖ Avoid alcohol and heavy meals before sleep
- ❖ Get regular exercise
- ❖ Before going to bed, avoid activities that stimulate your mind like watching TV/movie or working in computer or laptop, etc.
- ❖ Minimize noise, light, and excessive hot and cold temperatures where you sleep
- ❖ Develop a regular bed time and go to bed at the same time each night
- ❖ Try taking a hot bath or drinking a hot (non-caffeinated) drink, before going to bed.
- ❖ Do something quiet like listening soothing music
- ❖ You can also try some relaxation techniques like deep breathing, meditation, visualization, muscle relaxation etc.

AVOID MULTITASKING

Multitasking: an unavoidable feature of our 24/7 lifestyle. Multitasking is probably productivity's biggest enemy. Handling too many things at one time generally leads to forgetfulness. Unfortunately this has become a way of life of each individual be it a working woman or a housewife. A man also deals with a lot many things at the job front as well as at home. Even children handle studies, tuitions, sports, and

art or dance classes simultaneously. All this result in a less effective memory. Doing less and doing it without interruptions can be the key to being more productive.

In a University of Michigan study, participants who were asked to write a report and check email at the same time took one-and-a-half times longer than those who handled each task separately.

Stanford University psychology professor Clifford Nass provided research showing that chronic multi-taskers are even worse at multitasking than those who work on one task at a time.

Here are some tips to get rid of the effect of multitasking:

1. **Making a to-do list:** Not many people have a habit of making a list of task to be done during the day whereas it is the first step towards effective time management. Once your list is ready, you can plan your day accordingly which reduces stress. At the end of day when you see all the task done it gives you satisfaction.

2. **Prioritization:** Once your to-do list is ready, you have to prioritize your work according to their importance and urgency. You will realize that by doing just 20% of your tasks most of your urgent work is done. The rest 80% can be handled according to the time available or can be addressed at a later stage.

3. **Avoid distractions:** This means that you should concentrate only on the task at hand and avoid unnecessary distractions which may hamper your work. Like, turning off all phone and email notifications. Check your email at certain times, resisting the temptation to switch windows as soon as you receive a new one.

4. **Seek a quiet place to work:** This will result in finishing your task quickly as you will be able to concentrate better in a quiet environment.

5. **Organize your work place, reduce clutter:** It's hard to focus on a task when the other things are scattered across your home or workplace. If you are working on one subject or a project or even a recipe, keep only those things around which are related to it. Stack unnecessary things away.

6. **Schedule time for individual tasks:** Assign a particular time for each task and try to finish that task in the given time.

7. **Group similar tasks:** Similar kind of work should be done together. For example, shopping for grocery should be combined with shopping for stationary or getting some photocopies of documents etc. so that you don't have to go out again and again. Some task can be delayed, if possible, to accomplish similar tasks at one go.

SETTING CLEAR GOALS

The level of our concentration is in direct proportion to the intensity of our desire to remember. If we read something merely for the sake of reading it or to merely pass time, we may not remember it. But if we have a clear goal to remember something, we will always be able to do so.

Even if you have a clear set goal in your mind, concentration can sometimes become difficult if achieving that goal seems very difficult or an assignment appears overwhelming. In that case, try breaking down the big goal into smaller easily achievable goals, i.e., break down an assignment into more 'doable' tasks. For example, if you have to research a report, write it up, and present it; make researching a goal in itself. Once, this is done, the second step, outlining it, becomes easier. Writing it up become your third goal; and then finally, focus on the final step: presenting your findings. Broken down into four manageable chunks, it becomes easier for each one to be pursued with effortless concentration.

FORGETTING UNWANTED MEMORIES

One of the chief things causing interference with concentration is internal pollutants like anger, fear, doubts, jealousy, and bad memories, which cloud our mind most of the time. These can replace concentration with restless preoccupation and mental turmoil. To concentrate on a thing we need to clear these clouds. *For instance,* let's say you want to write on a slate or a paper. If something already written on it is not properly erased, then even if something good is later written on it, it will not be legible. So whatever is written on the slate or paper of mind must be thoroughly cleaned before you can write something on it again.

But the mind is such a wonderful slate or paper that whatever is written on it sinks so deeply within that to remove it is not so easier task. It is not easy to forget things. To erase what efforts do we have to do? How is erasing possible?

FORGIVE AND HAVE MERCY

To forget the mistakes of someone, you have to forgive and shower mercy on that person. Suppose a person behaves with you in a wrong manner, this act of his is pinching you frequently, the way the dust particle irritates you when it enters the eye. The influence of this has been engraved deep within you, layers upon layers. But if you inculcate the feeling of forgiveness and mercy, then you can forget it easily.

Another method to put an end to an issue or dispute physically or mentally in your mind is to fold two hands and beg for forgiveness by saying sorry.

If one person forgets the mistakes of others from his mind, it does not mean that he doesn't know what mistake the other person has done. It does not also mean that he is made of stone, i.e. he is insensitive. Rather he has acquired the strength to not be affected by an insult. It is also not the case that he is losing his dignity.

Rather, the style and the technique of his life is that of letting things go, of forgiving. Meditation helps to get this power to forgive and remain calm. **So the technique to forget is to forgive.**

DIVERT YOUR MIND TOWARDS SOMETHING DIFFERENT

Another method is to divert the mind towards some other direction, or to busy the mind with something else. Mostly people use the opposite technique when they get distressed: they pay more and more attention to the person who has behaved in a bad manner. They will keep thinking, *I will not leave this person; he has harassed and disturbed me a lot throughout my life.* So this negative memory then become more firm. How it can then be forgotten?

If you want to remember something or somebody, you have to recall it repeatedly. When children are being taught at school, they are asked to revise what they have learned again and again; only then are they able to remember it. It becomes firm in their memory. That is why, if you remember or pay attention to somebody's mistakes again and again, you will not be able to forget the mistake of that person; it firmly takes root in your memory; you will get sorrow and the duration of the pain will keep increasing. So what do you do? Divert your mind and attention from that issue to something else. You would have experienced in life that when your attention andtime are used in some specific task, old issues are be forgotten. So, when time has passed by, when something is not being repeatedly used, or when one's attention is engaged in something else, all old issuesare forgotten.

Meditation is the ultimate process to clean up your mind and enjoy your work.

MEDITATION

Meditation in other words means 'Attention Training'. Studies have shown that meditation helps improve attention thus helping people lead a more peaceful, content, and happy lives. It helps people to focus their attention on the present which in turn reduces their stress and worries.

HOW MEDITATION IMPROVES CONCENTRATION

'Thalamus' is known as the gatekeeper of senses. It funnels the sensory information *(smell, touch, sound etc.)* deeper in to the brain. If sensory information reaches the brain, only then do we become 'aware' of it and that information or the agent generating that information *disturbs* us. Meditation has been found to reduce the incoming information to a trickle. This means, we are able to *focus* on what we are doing i.e., concentrate unhindered. This is way meditation improves concentration.

MEDITATION IMPROVES CORTICAL THICKNESS

Scientists have found meditation is associated with a thicker cerebral cortex and more grey matter—i.e., the parts of the brain linked to memory, attention span, decision-making and learning. But it's not necessary to meditate silently for a year or so. One study found people who meditated at least once a week for four years showed increased cortical gyrification, the folding of the cerebral cortex that helps people process information.

WHAT IS MEDITATION?

Meditation is the process of empowering and recharging the mind by channelizing our thoughts in right direction while being in right consciousness of the self.

Meditation is not just focusing on a point or stopping all thoughts. The nature of the mind is to create thoughts. But many a times, while in stress or handling too many things, the number of thoughts coming to our mind increase so much that we find it difficult to think clearly and concentrate on one task at hand.

The process of mediation not only helps mind to relax by reducing the number of thoughts but also leads to attitudinal change by cleansing all negative and wasteful thoughts and consciously creating positive thoughts about the self and others. In simple words, meditation can be described as a three-step process:

1. Reflecting the self
2. Relaxing the mind
3. Recharging the mind

REFLECTING THE SELF

We spend most of our time observing others and thinking about them. We even judge ourselves on the basis of what others think about us. Meditation is an inner journey. In meditation, we sit comfortably, stop thinking about others, and start observing ourselves, who I am, what is my role in a particular relationship or a situation, how I am behaving, what kind of thoughts I am creating in response to the stimulus? So it's a step of self observation and introspection.

RELAXING THE MIND

After observing the thoughts, now channelize the flow of thoughts on the basis of right knowledge. Like a detached observer, check the thoughts you are creating and match them with the ones you should be creating in that particular time. Choose and discard the disturbing and negative/waste thoughts about yourself and others, thereby relaxing your mind by reducing their burden and choose what thoughts you should create.

RECHARGING THE MIND

With the right consciousness about yourself and your inner powers and strengths, now consciously make an effort to create right and positive thoughts and try to be in that consciousness. As you choose and create powerful and positive thoughts about yourself and others around you, you start feeling good and empowered, as if you are being recharged.

In meditation, we not only create positive thoughts, but also visualize them and try to be in that state of mind, experiencing it at the same time. Thus our faculties—**mind and intellect—work together, yielding better concentration**.

Our mind is like a garden. It's on us, whether we want to plant thorny bushes in it or beautiful fragrant flowers. Weeds and unwanted plants grow on their own. If we want flowers, then, we have to make effort to sow powerful, healthy seeds, take proper care of the plants, water them and take out the weeds on a regular basis. Similarly, if we want our mind to be powerful, we have to water it with good, powerful thoughts and clean the negative wasteful ones on a regular basis; Meditation helps us to do that, thus improving the quality of our thoughts, eventually leading to powerful mind.

If we consider ourselves stuck in the traffic of thoughts, then install a traffic signal of meditation and see the difference. The traffic signal can help you remember the above three steps of meditation as follows:

1. RED LIGHT—*Reflecting the self*: Stop everything outside and observe your thoughts inside.
2. YELLOW LIGHT—*Relaxing the mind*: Channelizing the thoughts: Check and Choose the right thoughts in the right way of thinking.
3. GREEN LIGHT—*Recharging the mind*: Conscious and continuous flow of positive thoughts

HOW TO MEDITATE WHEN YOU DON'T HAVE TIME?

In today's fast life we are too busy to take out time for ourselves. There's an easy way for that too. You don't have to take out special time for meditation. Whenever you get stuck in the traffic JAM of your own thoughts, apply the rule of J-A-M (Just-A-Minute).

'J-A-M'—a solution to distress and recharge your mind! It takes just-a-minute to transform your world. For example, you are going for an interview and thousands of thoughts are coming in your mind about whether I will be asked difficult or easy questions? What if I am not selected? What if I won't be able to answer something?, What will happen to my family? For how many more days I have to search for a good job? Am I capable of clearing the interview, etc. Instead of wasting your time and mental energy like this, take out a minute to *check, choose and change* your thoughts which empowers you and helps you to perform better. You can talk to yourself for a minute like this:

Like stars shine to bring light during the night, I am a spiritual being of radiant light, like a sparkling star in the night sky, reflecting and radiating spiritual light all around... I am a child of God, sent on this earth for a special purpose. The light which emanates from the heart of me is peaceful and loving... It touches each and everyone whomever I meet... Today I am going to appear for an interview. I am capable and will perform very well. I have no expectations, I know the best will happen to me... God has given me my own inner strengths and on the basis of that, I am going to perform very well today. Whatever the result is, I will accept it with grace and relaxed mind. I am happy and contented. I am going to remain happy... Happiness is my property and is going to remain with me no matter what... I know I can do it.

These thoughts will replace any disturbing or negative thoughts which might be coming in your mind. But the most important thing is taking out this one minute for yourself.

Here are a few thoughts or themes for meditation to help you:

❖ I am just a tiny point of pure energy, of light, situated at the center of the forehead. And within that tiny point lie all my thoughts, feelings, emotions, attitudes, beliefs and my personality traits. Within the point of light that I am, lie all the qualities of spirit that I have. I am a source of love, peace, power and wisdom for others.

❖ I am a miniscule point of energy, at the centre of the forehead and I am instrumental in making this body work. This body may be heavy and big as compared to me, but I, the soul, am so light, and free that I can almost fly. I experience bliss as the soul releases itself from the bondage of matter.

Online website links for learning meditation:
Visit this website **http://www.just-a-minute.org** updated with many useful meditation commentaries both for adults and children. There is also an option (for 'traffic-control') at the right top corner to play meditation commentary every hour or a chime every hour.

Learn Online Rajyoga Meditation to Enhance your Life and Relationships **http://learnmeditationonline.org**

Meditation for beginners: Essentials of Raja Yoga, **Discover the Spirit within** (28 mins) https://www. youtube.com/watch?v=DJOk99Q1Kmk

For a **good memory** proper diet, relaxation and exercise are required. In the same way for a **powerful mind,** a nutritious diet of good, positive thoughts, minimizing the thoughts to relax and generation of positivity is required as mind exercise. Meditation helps to achieve this target. It's the most important step to increase your concentration.

Answers to the brainteasers and puzzles:

1. MATCHSTICK PUZZLES:

(i)

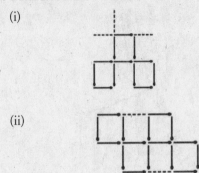

(ii)

2. (a) Niagara Falls   (b) Middle-aged
   (c) Too high   (d) Shut up sit down
   (e) For instance   (f) Too funny for words
   (g) Split personality   (h) Under World

3. Observation skills
   (i) 6 F, our brains are trained to overlook the word OF
   (ii) Unique item is: pencil

CHAPTER AT A GLANCE

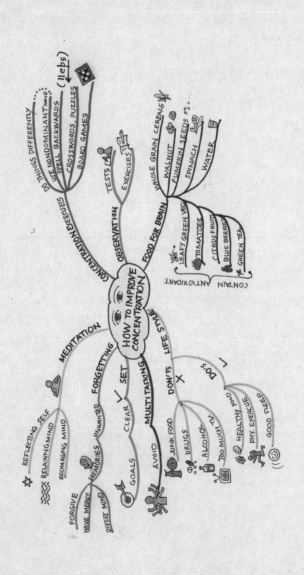

PART C

STUDENT SECTION

Every now and then we see people coming up with various techniques to help students get rid of exam phobia. Even then, memorizing everything in the syllabus is a big problem for many students.

Memory techniques have been proved to help students a great deal to memorize simple and abstract information in all subjects.

In this section, we try to provide memory solutions for various topics like learning to memorize:

- ❖ short and long answers,
- ❖ chemistry periodic table,
- ❖ formulae for chemical compounds,
- ❖ history dates,
- ❖ maths formulae,
- ❖ values of constants,
- ❖ biological terms,
- ❖ diseases and their symptoms, etc.

Other topics like memorizing vocabulary, foreign language, and general knowledge data including country–capitals, spellings, etc. have already been discussed in detail in the earlier *chapters 6, 7, 10 and 11* in Part B of the book.

Though different chapters in this section provide memory solutions for different subjects, we recommend that irrespective of your subject of interest, **you must refer to all the topics so as to understand the usage of memory techniques in various forms.**

You will notice that the techniques used to memorize history dates are the same as those being used to memorize chemistry periodic table or constants.

Our suggestion is you keep the earlier tricks in mind while reading this section so that you get the maximum exposure to different examples from different subjects. This will enable you to understand the application of memory techniques in your own studies in a better manner.

Memory techniques do not encourage rote-learning. Since these techniques are based on principles of association and visualization, it is important to understand the topic clearly, and only then will you be able to visualize it. Also understand that using memory techniques we do not memorize the answers word for word. Instead, these techniques work like clues to help you memorize and recall the keywords or the confusing part of the answers correctly. You can use different memory techniques for memorizing different topics as per your choice and comfort.

All the techniques and their uses are also tabulated *(in chapter 22—Smart Study Skills)* **for your easy reference along with their direct application in different questions.**

17

CHEMISTRY

A Chemistry student is required to memorize names of various elements of the periodic table, their valencies, compounds and alloys made by them, cause and effects of different kinds of chemical reactions, scientific names, and much more by heart. And even after repeating it several times, we cannot guarantee a perfect recollection, and if we don't repeat it, we become confused.

In this chapter, we will learn how memory techniques are useful in memorizing such difficult facts using the imagination and creativity of the brain.

MEMORIZING THE CHEMISTRY PERIODIC TABLE

There are 118 elements in the periodic table. I am yet to meet a Chemistry teacher who has memorized all the elements of the periodic table along with their atomic numbers.

But if you know the codes of the phonetic peg system well, you can memorize the complete periodic table in just a day or two. Sounds impossible? It's possible! Hundreds of my students have mastered this.

YOU CAN DO IT TOO

My son Devansh achieved this seemingly impossible task at a young age of five, when he did not even know the C of Chemistry. His name got registered in **the India Book of Records** as 'the youngest child to memorize the complete periodic table'.

How can one do it?

We can convert the abstract names of elements into images by using the PNN method and for learning atomic numbers, the phonetic peg system can be used. Once you have images for both element and atomic number, you need to make a funny association between them.

For example, the atomic number of **Zinc** is **30**

Zinc: Zinn (PNN)

30: Mess (Phonetic)

*Visualize that a **Zinn** is serving food to everybody in the **Mess** at a very fast rate.*

Below is a chart for your reference. This will help you memorize the complete periodic table:

Element	Symbol	At. No.	PNN of element	Phonetic Codes (At. No.)	Association
Hydrogen	H	01	Hydrogen Balloon	SuiT	A suit tied with many *hydrogen* balloons is flying in the air
Helium	He	02	Heel	SuN	Special is flying in the air *heels* to walk on the sun
Lithium	Li	03	Litchee (fruit)	SuMo	A sumo wrestler is eating lots of *litchees*
Beryllium	Be	04	Berry	SiR	*Sir* is distributing *berries* to everybody
Boron	B	05	Boroplus (cream)	SaLe	*Boroplus* cream is on *sale*
Carbon	C	06	Car + bun	SaGe	A *sage* is eating buns in a car

Element	Symbol	At. No.	PNN of element	Phonetic Codes (At. No.)	Association
Nitrogen	N	07	Night	SKy	*Sky* is black at *night*
Oxygen	O	08	Ox	SoFa	An *ox* is sitting on a *sofa*
Fluorine	F	09	Floor	SoaP	Washing *floor* with *soap*
Neon	Ne	10	Knee	DoSa	Eating *dosa* while keeping it on the knees

Visualize the above associations clearly 2–3 times to strengthen their impression on your brain.

Below are some more associations for memorizing the next 10 elements of the periodic table:

Element	Symbol	At. No.	PNN of element	Phonetic Codes (At. No.)	Association
Sodium	Na	11	Soda Water	DaD	*Dad* is drinking *soda water*
Magnesium	Mg	12	Maggi	DeN	Cooking *Maggi* in the den

Element	Symbol	At. No.	PNN of element	Phonetic Codes (At. No.)	Association
Aluminium	Al	13	Aloo (potato)	DaM	Instead of water, *aloo* is rolling down from the *dam*
Silicon	Si	14	Silly person	DR.	This *Dr.* is looking absolutely *silly*
Phosphorus	P	15	Fox/Fossil	DoL	A *fox* is playing with a *doll*
Sulphur	S	16	Cell with Fur	DiSH	Some special *cells* with *fur* all around are served in a *dish*
Chlorine	Cl	17	Clown/ Chlorine water (swimming pool)	DecK	Everybody is watching **clown** dancing on the **deck**
Argon	Ar	18	Gun	DwarF	A dwarf is pointing a gun at you
Potassium	K	19	Pot	TaP	A big pot with a tap

Element	Symbol	At. No.	PNN of element	Phonetic Codes (At. No.)	Association
Calcium	Ca	20	Calcium Sandoz	NoSe	New *Calcium Sandoz* tablets that can be inhaled through the nose

Revise the above visualizations and try to recall and write the atomic numbers of the following elements:

Element	Symbol	At. No.
Sodium	Na	
Lithium	Li	
Nitrogen	N	
Phosphorus	P	
Potassium	K	
Carbon	C	
Chlorine	Cl	
Neon	Ne	
Potassium	K	
Silicon	Si	

PRACTICE MAKES PERFECT

Now try to make your own associations for the following random elements with their atomic numbers:

Element	Symbol	At. No.	PNN of element	Phonetic Codes (At.No.)	Association
Titanium	Ti	22	Titanic	NuN	
Manganese	Mn	25	Mango	NaiL	
Silver	Ag	47	Silver	RacK	
Iodine	I	53	Iodex	LiMe	
Tungsten	W	74	Tongue	KaR	
Platinum	Pt	78	Plate	KoFee	
Gold	Au	79	Gold	KaP	
Radium	Ra	88	Radio	FiFa	
Einsteinium	Es	99	Einstein	Baby	

MEMORIZING FACTS ABOUT METALS

1. **LIQUID METALS**—Hg, Ga, Cs, Fr

    Hg: Mercury: Mercury Bulb

    Ga: Gallium: Gali (street)

    Cs: Cesium: Scissors

    Fr: Francium: Frock

    Visualization:

    You are sitting in a *gali* under a *mercury bulb*, cutting *frock* with a pair of *scissors* and dipping it in *liquid*.

2. **Element kept in water** is Phosphorus (P)

   Phosphorus—Fox with pores

   Visualization:

   A *Fox* with *pores* always lives under *water.*

3. **ELEMENTS IN A PERIOD:**

   Let's say you have to memorize elements in *Group I* of the periodic table:

GROUP I	PNN
Lithium	Lichee
Sodium	Soda Water
Potassium	Pot
Rubidium	Ruby (precious stone)
Cesium	Scissors
Francium	Frock

Visualization:

Numbers of a group can be visualized using the Rhyme method. So Group I can be associated with 'Sun'.

On the *Sun, Lichees* are growing. You pluck them and soak them in *soda water* in a big *pot.* After some time, as if by magic, it gets converted into a big *ruby.* You cut it into small pieces using a pair of *scissors* and paste it on your *frock.*

In your exams, when you will be asked about the elements in group-I, you can easily visualize and recall what the elements are doing on the sun and all the elements will come to your mind in the right sequence.

Try to do the same for memorizing the elements of Group II:

GROUP II	PNN
Berillium	
Magnesium	
Calcium	
Strontium	
Barium	
Radium	

Visualization:

_____

_____

_____

_____

4. **SOME ALLOYS**

(i) **BRONZE**—Copper + Tin

   Cu + Sn

   PNN   Cousin

   Visualization:

   My *cousin* won a *Bronze* medal in a race.

(ii) **GUNMETAL**—Cu + Sn + Zn

   PNN : Cousin + Zinn

   Visualization:

   A *Zinn* is pointing a *metallic gun* at my *cousin*.

(iii) **STAINLESS STEEL**—Carbon + Iron + Nickel + Chromium

Carbon	Iron	Nickel	Chromium
C	Fe	Ni	Cr
Car	Fenny		Crow

Visualization:

My *stainless steel car* got stuck in a *fenny*. A powerful *crow* pulled it out.

(iv) **ROSE METAL**—Pb + Bi + Zn + Cd

Lead	Bismuth	Zinc	Cadmium
Pb	Bi	Zn	Cd
Punjab	Bi pass Zinn		Cadbury Chocolate

Visualization:

On the *Punjab bi pass* road, a *Zinn* is giving a *rose along* with a *Cadbury* chocolate bar to everyone.

5. MELTING POINTS

(i) Melting point of Tin is 232° C

PNN	Phonetic
TIN	232
Tin-Tin (comic)	n m n
	Naman (boy name)

Visualization:

Naman is reading a *Tin-Tin* comic book with great care as it *melts* easily.

(ii) Melting point of Gold is 1063° C

PNN	Phonetic
GOLD	1 0 6 3
Gold Plate	d s j m
	dosa + jam

Visualization:

As soon as you put a hot *dosa* with jam stuffing on a golden plate, it starts *melting*.

6. BOILING POINT

Boiling point of **Oxygen** is 90.2° C

Oxygen	9 0 . 2
Ox	Bus + stop + duck
	(Phonetic) + (decimal) + (shape)

Visualization:

An Ox started boiling with anger when he saw that the bus stop was full of ducks.

7. CHEMICAL COMPOUNDS

(i) **WASHING SODA:** $Na_2 CO_3 . 10H_2O$

Washing Soda   – washing with soda water

Na_2 – Nana

CO_3 – Carbonate—Car + bonate(bonnet)

$10H_2O$ – 10 glasses of water

Visualization:

Nana is **washing** the *bonnet of a car* with *10 glasses of soda water*.

(ii) **WATER GLASS**—Sodium Silicate

$$Na_2 Si O_3$$

Na2   – Nana

Si   – Silly

O   – Ox

3   – tree (rhyme)

Visualization:

Nana is giving **water** in a **glass** to a *silly ox* sitting on a *tree*.

Thus memory techniques are useful in memorizing various formulae of chemical compounds, atomic number of elements, classification of periodic table in groups, their valencies, and composition of various alloys and results of different chemical reactions, and various facts about chemical compounds and their reactions.

18

MEMORIZING HISTORY DATES

Memorizing history dates have always been a nightmare for many. Using a combination of various mnemonics learnt in the earlier chapters, you can memorize them in a very funny way!

To memorize historical dates, we need to have an image of the historical event and that of the date. Create those images by understanding the following steps:

STEPS FOR MEMORIZING HISTORY DATES

1. **Visualize the event:**

   First visualize the historical event to be memorized using the PNN method, like the birth of Gandhiji, or the First World War, etc.

2. **Visualize the date:**

   The date consists of three parts—*date, month, and year*.

   (a) Date can be visualized using the number peg system, i.e.

   Dates *1–20* can be memorized using the *rhyme method*

   Dates *21–31* can be memorized using the *shape method* (where 1 to 11 codes of shape method can be taken for dates 21–31 of any month)

(b) Month can be memorized using month mnemonics as given in chapter 13, '**Memorizing Numerical Facts and Data**' under the section on *'Memorizing Birthdates'*.

(c) Year can be memorized by converting the year into images using the *Phonetic Peg System*.

3. **Make an association:**

   Visualize an association between the event and the date.

SOME EXAMPLES

1. **The 1st atom bomb hit Hiroshima on August 6th, 1945**

Hiroshima	: Hero
6	: sticks (rhyme)
August	: National Flag
1945	: Rail (phonetic)

   (The confusion is about the year only and not the century, so there is no need to convert the century part in such kind of dates.)

   Visualization: Somebody hit the *Hero* (Shahrukh Khan) with an *atom bomb*, but he kept standing with a *national flag* (August) on a *stick (6)* in his hand, on top of the *rail (1945)*.

2. **Dandi March was started by Gandhiji on March 12th, 1930**

Dandi March	: dandi (walking stick)
12	: Shelf (rhyme)
March	: Holi (festival)
1930	: mess (phonetic)

   Visualization: Gandhiji was marching with a *dandi* in his hand, but people took out the *Holi* colours (March) from the *shelf (12)* and smeared him with it, creating a *mess (1930)*.

3. **Alexander attacked India in 323 BC**

    Alexander   : Alexander King

    323   : m n m: my name (phonetic)

    BC   : Before Christ

    Visualization: When Alexander attacked India, he bowed before Christ (B.C.) and said loudly, '*My name* (323) is Alexander'.

Till now we have taken dates where the centuries are quite obvious and there is no need to associate them with any image. But if the dates are such that you need to memorize the centuries as well, you can use the colour coding system using which we assign a particular colour to a century. We see that colour specifically in our visualization, which enables us to remember the century while recalling it.

Below is a list of colours that you may use as century code colours.

Years	Colour Codes
1500	Yellow
1600	Brown
1700	Royal blue
1800	Fluorescent green
1900	Orange
2000	Pink

It's totally your choice which colour you want to give to a particular century, provided you keep it constant throughout.

Let's see some examples to make it clear:

4. **Battle of Haldighati was fought in 1576**

   Battle of Haldighati : People fighting with haldi (turmeric)

   1576   : Yellow + Kash

   Visualization: People wearing *yellow* dresses are fighting with *haldi* for *cash (76)*.

5. **Battle of Buxar was fought in 1764**

   Battle of Buxar   : Boxer fighting

   1764   : Royal Blue + jar

   Visualization: A *Boxer* wearing *royal blue* gloves is fighting while standing on a big *jar.*

6. **Treaty of Lahore was signed in 1846**

   Treaty of Lahore   : Treat in the Law house

   1846   : Brown + Raja

   Visualization: A *Raja* sitting on a *brown* throne is, giving *treat* to everybody *in the Law house* and signing on *brown* papers.

7. **Rabindranath Tagore got the Nobel Prize for literature in 1913.**

   Noble Prize   : Noble Prize

   Literature   : Books

   1913   : Orange + Dam

   Visualization: Rabindranath Tagore is putting all his *literary works (books) that are* covered in an *orange* cloth on the *dam* and getting a *Nobel Prize* for it.

Now practice some history dates by yourself:

1. C.V. Raman got the Nobel Prize for Physics in 1930 for his study of the scattering of light

2. Russian revolution took place in the year 1917

_____

3. Prarthana Samaj was established in the year 1867

_____

4. Death of Shahjahan was in the year 1666

_____

5. Birth of Subhash Chandra Bose was in the year 1897

_____

Memory techniques play a very important role in changing the perspective of a student towards boring and difficult subjects. Using these methods, memorizing history dates will become fun rather than a burden as it was earlier.

19

MEMORIZING ANSWERS OF SOCIAL STUDIES

MEMORIZING SHORT ANSWERS

You can memorize short answers using the following steps:

❖ Take out key words from your answers and
❖ Make a mental picture of those keywords using PNN
❖ Visualize them using the chain method

Let's take some examples from the school syllabus:

Q1. What are archives?

Ans. **Archives** are places where **manuscripts** are kept.

Archives   : Archies Gallery
Manuscripts   : Menu card

Visualization: In *Archies gallery, menu cards* are displayed instead of greeting cards.

Q2. What was the language of administration under the Delhi Sultans?

Ans. Persian was the language of administration under the Delhi Sultans.

Persian   : Pari (angel)

Visualiztion: Delhi Sultans speak the language of *Pari (angel)*.

Q3. From which country did Ibn Battuta travel to India?

Ans. Ibn Battuta travelled to India from Morocco.

Ibn Battuta	: Batuni Insaan *(talkative person)*
Morocco	: Mor *(peackock)*

Visualiztion: A *Batuni insaan (talkative person)* travelled to India sitting on a *mor (peacock)*.

Q4. In whose reign did the Sultanate reach its farthest extent?

Ans. In Muhammad Tughluq's reign the Sultanate reached its farthest end.

Tughluq : Tilak

Visualization: Sultan sabse farthest end par pahucha, to Muhammad ne use *Tilak* kiya.
(Muhammad gave a *Tilak* to the Sultan when he reached its farthest end).

Q5. What were the qualifications necessary to become a member of a committee of the sabha in the Chola empire?

Ans. To become a member of a committee of the sabha in the **Chola empire**, the following qualifications were necessary:

* The member had to be a **revenue-paying land owner**.
* He had to **possess** his own **home**.
* He had to be between the **age of 30–70 years**. .
* He should have been **honest**.
* He had to have **knowledge of the Vedas**.
* He should be well versed in **administrative matters**.

Visualization:

The keywords are highlighted in the answer above.

Imagine a person nominated for making a new committee representing people who cook *chole* for the entire empire. He is giving reasons why he should be elected.

Imagine he is standing in front of his house and saying 'I **own** this **house** and **pay revenue** for it. When I initially came here, it was all a **mess (30)**. Now it's such a nice place that you can even **kiss (70)** it. I have been very **honest** these days and want to spread this **knowledge** to all, so I want to become the **admin** of this new committee. Please vote for me'.

Q6. Name three types of rainfall?

Ans. Convectional rainfall, Orographic rainfall, and Cyclonic rainfall are the three types of rainfall.

Conventional	: Convincing
Orographic	: Oro (name)
Cyclonic	: Cycle

Visualization: Since it is raining, *Oro* is *convincing* his parents to allow him to ride the *cycle* in the rain.

Q7. What is the 'Doctrine of Lapse'? Explain with examples.

Ans. The **Doctrine of Lapse** declared that if an Indian ruler died without a **male heir**, his kingdom would 'lapse', that is, become part of the company territory. One kingdom after another was **annexed** simply by applying this doctrine: **Sambalpur (1850)**, **Udaipur (1852)**, **Nagpur (1853)**, and **Jhansi (1854)**.

Visualization: Visualize that a **Doctor** *(Doctrine)* is saying if you don't have a male baby in your **lap** *(Lapse)*, then your kingdom will become part of the company. See as if he is saying 'NEXT' *(annexed)* and one after another, kingdoms are becoming part of his company.

After coming out of his room one person is saying: '**Sambhal kar** *(Sambalpur),* **udne** *(Udaipur)* wala **naag** *(Nagpur),* sabko apne **jhanse** *(Jhansi)* mein fasa raha hain.'

(*'Beware, a flying snake is trying to trap everyone in its decoy'*).

MEMORIZING LONG ANSWERS

You can memorize long answers using the following steps:

- ✤ Just break your long answers into small sentences.
- ✤ Take a key word from each sentence and associate it with any of the pegs system.
- ✤ Make a mental picture of that association.
- ✤ While recalling, just recall the pegs and you will be able to give the whole answer correctly without missing a single point.

Let's take some examples from the school syllabus:

Using the Number Rhyme Peg System

Q8: Narrate the achievements of RajendraChola.

Ans. Rajendra succeeded his father Rajaraja-I and carried in the aggressive policy. He conquered the whole of Sri Lanka. He overran the Chalukyas of Vengi. He took his kingdom upto Central India. He then overran the whole of Orissa and Bengal right up to the Southern banks of the Ganga. He then annexed the islands of Lakshadweep and Maladweep. He also humbled the Sri Vijya kingdom which included the Malay Peninsula and Sumatra.

The naval supremacy helped him build a vast maritime empire to control trade and commerce. Indian ships began to sail through the straits of Malacca. He also conquered Java and some other eastern islands.

Memory Solution:

Break the answer into several small sentences, as shown below, and identify the key words in each sentence.

- **Rajendra** succeeded his **father Rajaraja-I** and carried in the **aggressive** policy.
- He **conquered** the whole of **Sri Lanka**.
- He overran the **Chalukyas of Vengi**.
- He took his kingdom up to **Central India**.
- He then overran the whole of **Orissa** and **Bengal** right up to the Southern **banks of the Ganga.**
- He then annexed the islands of **Lakshadweep** and **Maladweep.**
- He also humbled the Sri **Vijya** kingdom which included the Malay Peninsula and Sumatra.
- The **naval supremacy** helped him build a vast maritime empire to **control trade and commerce.**
- **Indian ships** began to sail through the **straits** of **Malacca.**
- He also **conquered Java** and some other eastern islands.

Visualize the answer point wise while associating with the rhyming pegs as given below:

1. **Sun:** Raja *(Rajendra)* and his father double Raja *(Raja Raja-I)* went to visit Sun and due to its heat became aggressive.
2. **Shoe:** Wearing the magical shoes, he conquered Ravan *(Sri Lanka).*
3. **Tree:** A chalu *(Chalukyas)* behanji *(vengi)* is running on a tree.

4. **Door:** He built doors up to Central India.

5. **Hive:** He ran and started doing the Orissa dance *(Orissa)* wearing bangles *(Bengal)*, *near a hive* on the banks of Ganga river.

6. **Sticks:** He hit everyone with sticks and got the islands of Lakshman *(Lakshdweep)* and Mala *(Maladweep)*.

7. **Lemon:** He achieved vijay *(Vijya)* and wore the garland of lemons.

8. **Plate:** He controlled trade and commerce with the help of an oval *(naval)* supreme *(supremacy)* plate.

9. **Line:** Indian ships made a line to sail through streets *(staits)* of the actress Malaika Arora *(Malacca)*.

10. **Hen:** Hen is working on the computer to conquer Java. (language).

Q9. Describe the layers of the atmosphere.

Ans. Our atmosphere is divided into five layers which, starting from earth's surface, are the following:

1. **Troposphere**—most of the **changes in the weather** occur in this layer.

2. **Stratosphere**—it provides **ideal flying conditions** for large jet airplanes. It has also a rich **layer of ozone** which absorbs harmful ultra-violet radiations from sun.

3. **Mesosphere**—**Meteoroids entering** from the space burn up in this layer.

4. **Thermosphere**—in this layer **temperature rises** very rapidly with height. This layer helps in **radio transmission**.

5. **Exosphere**—Air **density is very low** in this layer and it is merged in the inter-planetary space.

Hint: The first point can be memorized as:

Troposphere can be visualized as a trophy. Visualize that sun is holding a trophy which is causing changes in the weather.

Other key points have been set in bold for you. You have to associate the points with the corresponding rhyming codes.

Your memory visualization for the above:

1. _____
2. _____
3. _____
4. _____
5. _____

Using Chain Method

Q10. What are the main functions of a Municipal Corporation?

Ans. A Municipal Corporation performs a lot of functions. It is responsible for:

1. Water and electricity supply.
2. Maintaining roads and street lights.
3. Maintaining gardens, parks, and beauty of the city.
4. Running schools, hospitals, and health centres.
5. Sanitation and control spreading of diseases.
6. Garbage collection and disposal etc.

Memory Solution: To memorize the above answer, we make the PNN of Municipal Corporation as follows and then form a chain of all the points in the answer and visualize them simultaneously.

The PNN for **municipal** can be *munimji* and for **corporation**, it can be *corporate people*. So the scene you can create is that some corporate people are coming to investigate and **munimji** is supposed to make all the arrangements. In order to impress the **corporate** people, he arranged for:

- ❖ Proper **water and electrical supply** in the area.
- ❖ With electricity supply, he arranged for **road and street lights**.
- ❖ Fancy street lights are placed in the **gardens and parks** to enhance their beauty.
- ❖ In the gardens, **schools and hospitals** are opened.
- ❖ In the hospitals, to **control the spread of diseases**, proper **sanitation** and **garbage collection** are taken care of.

You see by connecting the entire key points together in a chain, it becomes very easy to memorize all the 6 points in a sequence, without forgetting any point.

Now you can try the following question yourself in the same way:

Q11. How are mountains useful to us?

Ans.   Mountains are very useful to man. Some common benefits are:

1. They are the **storehouse** of water.
2. Mountain **glaciers** are the **source of perennial rivers**.
3. Many **fresh water lakes and springs** originate from there.
4. The valleys and slopes are used for **cultivation**.
5. Mountains have a rich variety of **flora and fauna**.
6. **Reservoirs** on rivers are used for **generating hydroelectricity**.

7. **Forests** on mountains are a good **source of fuel, fodder, gums, and raisins**.

8. Mountains are **good tourist's spots** and are known for adventure sports.

> Hint: The key points have been set in bold for you. You have to make a chain of all the points while visualizing the same.

Your memory visualization for the above:

_____
_____
_____
_____
_____
_____
_____

Using the Hide-and-Seek Method

Q12. What were Mahatma Gandhi's views on English education? Why did he want to teach children handicrafts?

Ans: Mahatma Gandhi, one of the greatest leaders of India, had his own views on education.

1. He held the view that **colonial education** would create **a sense of inferiority in the minds of Indians**. It would make them think that **Western civilization was superior** and destroy the pride that they had in their culture.

2. According to him, Western education focused on reading and writing rather than on oral knowledge; **it valued textbooks rather than lived experience and practical knowledge**.

3. He believed education in English would cripple Indians, **distancing them from their own social surroundings.**

4. He strongly felt that **Indian languages** ought to be the medium of instruction because this would **make it easier for them to understand** the whole thing and would enable them to **recover their sense of dignity and self-respect.**

5. Mahatma Gandhi laid **emphasis on learning a craft** as it would make them work with their own hands and get a **practical knowledge** of the whole thing. By doing so they would learn how different things operated. The learning of a craft would develop not only their mind but also their capacity to understand. Later on such a thing could **help many to earn their own living.**

Hint: The key points have been set in bold for you. You have to associate the points with the stops in your route or location.

Memory Solution:

Suppose the route of your classroom is as follows:

- ✤ Door
- ✤ Poster
- ✤ Chair
- ✤ Blackboard
- ✤ Window

Now the points in the above answer can be linked with the stops in your classroom as:

1. Door: The **colony** of **Indians** is considered **inferior**, so they are not allowed to enter through the door to get education.

Only people belonging to a **superior western civilization** can go in.

2. Poster: The boy in the poster is suggesting the use of **only textbooks, no practical knowledge.**

3. Chair: As the teacher sits on the chair, it starts flying and takes her to a **distance away from her own social surroundings.**

Now try to associate the remaining 2 points of the answer in the same way:

4. Blackboard: _____
    _____

5. Window: _____
    _____

Since the hiding places are unlimited, a lot many questions can be easily memorized using the hide-and-seek method. Also, chain method and other pegging methods are equally helpful in memorizing different kinds of answers. After visualizing the associations strongly in your mind for 2–3 times, the answers will be embedded deep in your memory. Revising answers, memorized by these methods, take much shorter time.

MIND MAPS. REMEMBER?

Long answers and whole chapters can also be summarized using the smart note making technique of 'Mind Maps' learnt in chapter 15, 'Mind Maps–Creative Note Making', which will help you not in just summarizing but also in memorizing the notes.

20

MATHS AND PHYSICS

Maths and Physics are logical subjects. In such subjects, we need to understand the concepts to solve the problems and practice each concept thoroughly. To find the solution to problems, we also need to make use of certain formulae. Most of the times, students get confused or forget the formulae. In case we totally forget the formula, we generally try to recollect it, if possible, by using certain logic or understanding about the topic.

For example, if a student forgets the formula of the volume of cylinder, which is $\pi r^2 h$, he may recall it from the knowledge that

	Volume	= Area of base × height
So,	Volume of cylinder	= Area of circle × height
Therefore,	Volume of cylinder	= $\pi r^2 h$

So, understanding the concept is important in Mathematics, but if you get confused in some formulae or are not able to apply any logic to recall, you can make use of the creativity of memory techniques to memorize the confusing part or even the complete formula.

MEMORIZING PLACE VALUE

Remembering number of zeroes in place value chart is very difficult and confusing for most of the students. Here is a chart showing some mnemonics to memorize it:

PLACE VALUE CHART

PLACE VALUE	PNN	NUMBER OF 0'S	NUMBER PEG (Shape)	VISUALIZATION
Lakh	Lake	10^5	Hook	People are crossing the lake using a hook
Crore	Crorepati (KBC Show)	10^7	Axe	Amitabh Bachchan is carrying an axe on the show
Million	Mili (Girl)	10^6	Hockey stick	Milli is playing with a hockey stick
Billion	Bill Gates	10^9	Balloon	Bill Gates is blowing a balloon
Trillion	Three Lion	10^{12}	Shelf (rhyme peg)	Three lions are jumping on a shelf

MEMORIZING METHOD FOR MEASUREMENT UNITS

Measurement units in sequence are:

Kilogram Hectogram Dekagram Gram Decigram Centigram Milligram

We can memorize this sequence using the following *Acrostic*:
King Henry Died Unexpectedly Drinking Chocolate Milk

King   Kilo (1,000)
Henry   Hecta (100)
Died   Deka (10)

Unexpectedly	(Unit of measurement – it can meter, gram, litre)
Drinking	Deci (1/10)
Chocolate	Centi (1/100)
Milk	Milli (1/1,000)

This acrostic helps a lot while converting the measurement from one unit to another.

MEMORIZING MATHEMATICAL FORMULAE

VISUALIZING SYMBOLS

It involves learning some imagery that is associated with mathematical symbols. The following table presents ideas for some common symbols. You don't have to use the images of the following table if there are others that work better for you.

Mathematical Symbol	Image
+ (add)	Ambulance/Nurse (with a red cross on her hat)
- (subtract)	Negative emotion (anger/villain/submarine/basement)
X (multiply or times)	Fence/knitting needles
/ (divide)	Slide
√ (square root)	Bus stand/ tree root/under a tent
π (pi)	A pie (the kind you eat)
∫ (integral)	Violin (violins have integral shaped cutouts on each side)

Mathematical Symbol	Image
Σ (sum)	Summer/jaw of animal symbolizing 'sum'
= (equals)	Sandwich (two parallel slices of bread)/railway track
((open bracket)	Imagine a flower opening (since flowers generally don't close)
) (close bracket)	Mousetrap (since mouse traps are designed to close)

Apart from the symbols given above, you can also create images for other symbols that you may need.

Here are some common formulas and suggested memory mnemonics. The mnemonics presented here use a combination of the alphabet peg system for remembering letters, the phonetic mnemonic system for remembering numbers, and the images from the above table for remembering the mathematical symbols. If you want, you can also use the numbers from the numeric peg system for remembering numbers.

MEMORIZING QUADRATIC EQUATION FORMULA

Let's look at the quadratic formula first.

$$x = \frac{-b \pm \sqrt{b^2 - 4ac}}{2a}$$

Going from left to right, I turn the formula into a story or scene, taking each number and symbol as a character in the story.

❖ *x* is an *x-ray fish*; I can see right through its skin to its skeleton.

- ❖ It is raining heavily. The *x*-ray fish is floating in water. The fishcomes on the *road* (= sign).
- ❖ There it sees an *angry* (– sign) *bear* (b).
- ❖ Bear is *confused* (±) where to go.
- ❖ He seesa *bus stand* ($\sqrt{\ }$) and decidesto move there.
- ❖ On the bus stand another *bear* is already standing with *2* kids on his shoulder (b^2).
- ❖ Besides this there are*4 apes and a catfighting* with each other (–4ac).
- ❖ The bus came and *2 apes* came from under the bus stop ($\frac{\ }{2a}$) and boarded the bus.

Try to visualize this as clearly as possible using all your senses. Clearly imagine the location, the clouds above, the smell of the sand, and the sound of rainwater. Hear the noise of apes and cats fighting, the sound of bus. The more clearly you imagine the scene—as if you were actually there—the easier it will be to recall it.

Yes, going through this process takes time, but if you fully imagine it, you will find it unforgettable! Unforgettable means less study for you. It actually saves time! The same process works for memorizing any formula or equation.

MEMORIZING TRIGONOMETRY FORMULAE

Usually when trigonometry is introduced to students, they start mugging up all the ratios and that's why it become difficult for some students and they develop a phobia for such interesting concepts at the initial stage.

To memorize the **trigonometry ratios**, you just need to memorize this acrostic:

Some people have curly brown hair turned permanently black

That's all you need to memorize to register the trigonometry ratios in your mind forever. So here you go,

Some People Have
  S = P/H
  Sin = Perpendicular / Hypotenuse

Curly Brown Hair
  C = B/H
  Cos = Base/Hypotenuse

Turned Permanently Black
  T = P/B
  Tan = Perpendicular/Base

There are 3 more ratios: Cosec, Sec, and Cot. For these, just remember that:
  Cosec is the reciprocal of Sin; or **Cosec** = 1/Sin = H/P
  Sec is the reciprocal of Cos; or **Sec**= 1/Cos = H/B
  Cot is the reciprocal of Tan; or **Cot**= 1/Tan = B/P

Some more formulae from trigonometry:

Formula: Sin 3A = 3 SinA– 4 Sin³A

We can convert the formula into some story using the following codes:

  Sin   : Sushmita Sen
  3   : tree (rhyme)
  A   : Apple (alphabet peg)
  – 4   : 4 bad boys

Visualization:

Sushmita Sen *(Sin)* climbs a tree *(3)* to pluck apples *(A)*. As she was trying to jump on other side *(=)*, she gets trapped between tree and apples *(3 Sin A)*. Suddenly four bad boys *(–4)* came and put Sushmita Sen under the tree *(Sin³)* and ran away with the apples *(A)*.

Note: If you have confusion in one part only, then make association for just that, not the whole formulae.

MEMORIZING SQUARE ROOTS

1. $\sqrt{2}$ =   1.414
   $\sqrt{2}$ =   shoe (rhyme peg)
   1.414 =   r d r = radar

Visualization: You are using a radar to locate your shoes in the house.

2. $\sqrt{3}$ =   1.732
   $\sqrt{3}$ =   tree (rhyme peg)
   1.732 =   kmn = kumon classes

Visualization: You are taking Kumon class under a tree.

3. $\sqrt{5}$ =   2.236
   $\sqrt{5}$ =   hive (rhyme peg)
   2.236 = n m j = no match

Visualization: There is no match today as there is a big hive on the pitch

Note: The part before the decimal is already known by simple mathematical logic, so apply the technique in the confusion part only.

In the same way, you can memorize square, cubes, cube roots and reciprocals.

One of our students, *Himmat Bhardwaj*, has made a national record by memorizing all the square roots, cube roots, and reciprocals of all numbers from 1 to 100 upto 12 decimal places, using the above techniques. He also memorized square and cubes of numbers upto 100.

MEMORIZING PHYSICS CONSTANTS

1. **Mass of electron = 9.11×10^{-31} kg**

Electron = Electral Powder
9.11 = b d d = Buddha
−31 = mat (going down for negative sign)

Since the student knows how to write in the notation form, there is no need to memorize the place of decimal point, which always come after the first digit and is multiplied by powers of 10. So here we are memorizing the confusing part, i.e. the constant value and the degree of 10.

Visualization:

Visualize that *Buddha* (911) is meditating under a tree for a very long period, so you offered him to drink *electral powder* in water. As soon as he drinks it, his *mat* (31) descends *down* (−) because of breaking his fast.

2. **Mass of earth = 5.98×10^{24} kg**

5.98 = l p f = lap of
24 = Nehru *(phonetic peg)*

Visualization: Visualize a picture where a model of the earth is placed in the *lap of* (598) *Nehru* (24) and he is trying to weigh it.

Though only some formulae and constants have been discussed here, you may apply the same principles to other formulae.

Not all formulae are confusing and difficult, and the area of confusion may also vary from student to student. You should create your own list of formulae in which you have confusion and can make use of memory techniques to overcome it. As already mentioned, Mathematics is a subject of regular practice, so you need to do enough practice to retain it for a longer time.

21

BIOLOGY

Q1. What are the major groups of microorganisms?

Ans.: There are five major groups of microorganisms:

(i) **Bacteria:** They are single-celled disease-causing microorganisms. They can be spiral or rod-shaped.

(ii) **Fungi:** They are mostly multicellular disease-causing microbes. Bread moulds are common examples of fungi.

(iii) **Protozoa:** They mainly include organisms such as *Amoeba, Plasmodium,*etc. They can be unicellular or multicellular.

(iv) **Virus:** Viruses are disease-causing microbes that reproduce only inside the host organism.

(v) **Algae:** They include multicellular, photosynthetic organisms such as *Spirogyra, Chlamydomonas*, etc.

Memory Solution:

You can memorize all five microorganisms using the **shape and PNN** method as shown below:

1. *Candle* (1): Visualize that you are making use of a **candle** in your hand to see the *back, tea area (bacteria)*. The tea leaves are either *spiral or rod-shaped*.

2. *Duck (2):* Visualize that ***multiple funny guys*** (fungi–multicellular) are coming out of the mouth of a **duck** and as soon as they come out, they start eating rotten ***bread***.

3. *Heart (3):* Deep inside your **heart**, you cherish ***photos of zoo*** *(protozoa)*. In the zoo, you saw ***one*** tree of ***ambi*** *(amoeba)* and ***many plasma TVs*** *(multicellular plasmodium)* on it.

4. *Chair (4):* On a **chair**, a person with high ***viral fever*** (virus) is sitting inside the ***host's*** house.

5. *Hook (5):* ***All guys*** *(algae)* are ***photo-sensitive*** *(photosynthetic)*, so you hang them on a **hook** to click their photo.

Q2. Write the order of taxonomy in biology.

Ans. Kingdom, Phylum, Class, Order, Family, Genus, Species

Memory Solution:

Acrostic: *Kids Prefer Cheese Over Fried Green Spinach.*

Q3. Name the five kingdoms in which the organisms are grouped.

Ans. All living organisms are divided into five kingdoms, namely Monera, Protista, Fungi, Plantae, and Animalia.

Memory Solution:

Let's give all five kingdoms nicknames using the PNN method so that they become meaningful images and then connect them with each other in a meaningful sentence.

Monera: *Monica* (name of a girl)
Protista: *Protest*
Fungi: *Fun*
Plantae: *Plants*
Animalia: *Animals*

Visualization:

Visualize a girl named **Monica protesting** to have **fun** with **plants** and **animals**.

Q4. What are the main features of vertebrata?

Ans. These animals have a true **vertebral column** and are **bilaterally symmetrical**. All chordates possess the following features:

(i) have a **notochord**
(ii) have a **dorsal nerve** cord
(iii) are **triploblastic**
(iv) have paired **gill pouches**
(v) are **coelomate**

Memory Solution:

The bold words are the keywords, which can be visualized using the PNN and Chain Method as follows:

✤ **notochord**	:	no chord
✤ **dorsal nerve**	:	nerve connected to door
✤ **triploblastic**	:	triple blast
✤ **gill pouches**	:	fishes (gills) in pouches
✤ **coelomate**.	:	college mate

Visualization:

Vertebrata can be visualized as the backbone of any person.

Visualize that a doctor is demonstrating the **vertebra** (backbone) of a man to his students. He shows that it is **vertically placed** in the body and **symmetrical** on both sides. It is **no**t connected with any **chord**, so one of the **nerves** is connected to a **door**. Suddenly it blasts three times (**triple blasts**) and as a result **fishes** came out in **pouches**. These fishes are all **college mates**.

Q5. Explain how animals in Vertebrata are classified into further subgroups.

Vertebrates are grouped into five classes.

1. Pisces
2. Amphibia
3. Reptilia
4. Aves
5. Mammalia

Memory Solution:

These five classes can be summarized in an Acronym: **PARAM**.

Since a student already knows his subject matter, and is very well aware of these words, he only needs a clue to be able to recall it fast without missing any point, so this acronym will serve the purpose very well.

MEMORIZING DISEASES AND THEIR SYMPTOMS

Let's say you have to memorize that '**Hypothyroidism**' has the following signs and symptoms:

- Puffy face
- Weight gain
- Constipation
- Feeling cold
- Poor hearing
- Hair fall
- Muscle aches and stiffness
- Pain in joints
- Fatigue (tiredness)
- Weakness
- Poor memory and concentration

Memory Solution:

Since a student of the subject must know that **hypothyroidism** is a condition marked by low activity of the thyroid gland, which is present in the throat area, you can visualize a lady wearing a band around her neck, with '**low activity**' written on it.

To link the signs and symptoms of the disease, visualize that the lady, who is very **fat** (weight gain) and has a **puffy face**, came to your house. You asked her 'Why you are so fat?' She said 'I am fat because of **constipation**.' Outside she was feeling very **cold**, so you invited her inside. As soon as she comes inside, she started dancing very fast. You asked her repeatedly to stop, but she couldn't listen to what you were saying because of her **poor hearing**. Suddenly her **hair** started **falling** all around. Seeing that, she stopped but now her **muscles** were **aching** badly. They became very **stiff**; she started feeling severe **pain in** her **joints**. She was feeling very **tired and weak**, so you asked her where her home is, but she couldn't tell as she had **lost** her **memory**.

You can visualize all the above symptoms in this funny way on any person you may know who is suffering from hypothyroidism. Once you have visualized this clearly on someone, the moment you think about that person, all the symptoms will come to your mind without any confusion and will bring a smile to your face.

In the same way you can make visualizations of different disease symptoms and memorize them easily.

Many Biology topics can be very well summarized in creative and colourful mind maps, discussed in the chapter of mind mapping and also in next chapter on study skills. These will help you to have a whole topic or chapter at a glance. These notes will also help you revise things very fast.

2 2

SMART STUDY SKILLS

Students generally study just for the night before an assignment is due or the night before an exam. It's never too early or too late to develop good study habits. The sooner you get into a good study groove, the easier everything will be, and the better your chances of getting good marks.

Any skill which boosts a person's ability to study and pass exams with excellent scores can be termed a study skill. Study skills are discrete techniques that can be learned, usually in a short time, and applied to all or most fields of study.

Now-a-days, the most limited resource for everyone is time, especially for students who not only have to perform well in academics in this highly competitive world, but also excel in other activities. Good time management is the key to achieving academic success. We need to learn to effectively use our time so that we can achieve the best results in a limited period of time.

USEFUL STUDY SKILLS FOR OPTIMUM UTILIZATION OF TIME

- ❖ Smart Goal Setting
- ❖ PQRST Approach
- ❖ Mind Map Your Notes
- ❖ Use Memory Techniques
- ❖ Revise Scientifically

❖ Avoid Procrastination And Distractions
❖ Exam Tips

SMART GOAL SETTING

WHY GOAL SETTING?

Goal setting is important to channelize your energy, time, resources, and ideas into achieving something that is useful and meaningful in life. Without a target or a goal in our mind, important resources can go waste.

Clearly written goals enhance success. Although your main goals right now are most likely related to education and career, you may also want to set personal and relationship goals. Goals can be of 2 types: long-term goals and short-term goals.

➢ **Long-term goals** *(1–5 years goals):* Goals that you want to achieve in the future and that will take a few years' time (roughly about 1 to 5 years) to accomplish.

➢ **Short-term goals:** Tasks that help you work toward meeting one or more long-term goals or things you can accomplish today or this week or the next month). It can help you focus and work efficiently.

SET 'SMART' GOALS

❖ Specific: Goals should be defined in specific and clear terms.
❖ Measurable: It should be measurable so that you will know when you have achieved it. 'I will improve my vocabulary by end of this year' is not a measurable goal as improvement means

different things to different people. Rather the goal should be 'I will learn 1000 new words in the next 12 months.'

✦ Achievable: The goals should be achievable and realistic according to your resources and capabilities, otherwise non-fulfillment of goals becomes disheartening. For example, if you are getting 50 percent marks in an exam, don't target to achieve 100 percent directly in upcoming exams which is just a month ahead. Keep a more realistic target keeping on mind your own capabilities and motivation. Though 100 percent will be your final target, you should try to reach it step by step.

✦ Relevant: You should have a clear relevance of achieving that goal in your life. Don't get affected by others people's goals. Just because your friend decided to lose 5 kilos, it doesn't mean you should also aim for it. See if you really want to do it or is it just because of peer pressure.

✦ Timed: It should be time bound.

e.g., *'I will finish my assignment by 4.00 pm Tuesday.'* is a **SMART goal**.

e.g., *'I want to spend more time with my family'* is **not a SMART goal**. It's vague, immeasurable, and lacks a time limit.

Record your *(SMART)* goals in a table where one column is for *long-term goals* and another is for *short-term goals*. Some examples are given below:

Long–term Goals	Short–term Goals
Graduate with first division	Completing assignment for this semester by next Sunday
Buy own house (2BHK, 700 sq. ft) in Gurgaon, by January 2017	Finish revision of Chemistry in the next 10 days

Long–term Goals	Short–term Goals
Going to the US for work by March 2015	Limit my internet time to 2 hrs/day by next Saturday

PQRST APPROACH

While reading any information or chapter and making notes out of it, one approach which is highly recommended to make the best use of the first learning time is PQRST method. This method prioritizes the information in a way that relates directly to how they will be asked to use that information in an exam.

PQRST is an acronym for **P**review, **Q**uestion, **R**ead, **S**ummarize, **T**est. PQRST stands for five steps that you should use when reading something that you want to remember. These five steps are:

1. PREVIEW:

The first step, *preview*, advises that one should resist the temptation to read the whole book or chapter and instead glance through it in order to identify headings, sub-headings, and other outstanding features in the text like graphics, boxed text, etc. This is in order to identify ideas and formulate questions about the content of the chapter. *For example*, when you take an overview of a chapter on '*Principles of management*', you will notice that it talks about Fayol's 14 main principles. And by just going through the headings you will know the gist of the chapter.

2. QUESTION:

Formulate questions about the content of the reading. For example, convert headings and sub-headings into questions, and then look for answers in the content of the text. Other more general questions may also be formulated:

> *What is this chapter about?*

➤ *What question is this chapter trying to answer?*

➤ *How does this information help me?*

➤ *What must I remember about it?*

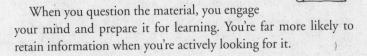

When you question the material, you engage your mind and prepare it for learning. You're far more likely to retain information when you're actively looking for it.

3. READ:

You should read through the related material, focusing on the information that best relates to the questions formulated earlier.

For example: If I am reading about a war, I will ask questions like *When? Where? Why? Between whom?etc.*

Now while reading the text, you must answer these questions before moving on. This way your complete concentration will be on the text that you are reading.

Do some underlining or highlighting of key words. Don't overdo it! If you want to take notes, read the whole section first, and then summarize it later.

4. SUMMARIZE:

The student summarizes the topic, bringing his or her own understanding into the process. Using key word or phrases, one is meant to identify major points and answers to questions from the questioning step. This may include **written notes, spider diagrams, flow diagrams, mind maps®, labelled diagrams, mnemonics, or even voice recordings.** Check back against the text, and note the things you missed out.

An example of summarizing a topic through a mind map is demonstrated in the next section of mind mapping your notes.

5. TEST:

So now you have finished the chapter (or a major section if the chapter contains large dissimilar sections). Test yourself and answer the questions drafted earlier, avoiding adding any questions that might distract or change the subject. Review all the material. If you made notes, read through these. Think about the relevance of what you learnt and how it all fits together. Reread any chapter summaries. Even though you have only just read the chapter, now is the **best** time to test yourself.

Researchers have tested this method and found it really helpful in improving readers understanding, and his/her ability to recall information. Summarizing is particularly effective if done properly, as is the questioning step. After all, this makes sense because it is putting your brain into gear and warming it up before you start.

MIND MAP YOUR NOTES

WHY SHOULD ONE TAKE NOTES?

Note-taking activity is one of the most crucial parts of learning. Taking effective notes during lectures or reading helps you to concentrate, stimulates your ability to recall, and helps you to be organized.

Students many a times think it is a boring and time-consuming activity and therefore revise directly from the textbook. However, if we have quality notes, we can save our time in revision and can in fact revise more number of times in the same duration as revising directly from the book.

Note taking helps students in:

❖ Extending their attention spans and keeps them focused.
❖ Learning more effectively by using both listening and writing skills.

- Selecting important material and discarding unimportant material.
- Changing from passive learners to active learners.
- Organizing the ideas they are learning.

Differences between note taking in lectures and when reading

The big difference between note taking in lectures and note taking from reading is that in lectures, you can't slow down or pause the lecturer if you fall behind your note taking. So, for taking notes we need to follow some strategies:

TAKING NOTES IN LECTURES

1. Think about the subject of the lecture beforehand so as to grasp the ideas quickly.
2. Concentrate on the 'big picture' in a lecture and do not try to write everything down.
3. Keep your notes brief—long notes do not help your understanding of the lecture at all.
4. Use your own abbreviations.
5. Make keywords stand out—underline, capitals.

TAKING NOTES FROM READING

1. Before you start reading, identify the purpose of reading.
2. Use your own words, wherever possible, to help understanding.
3. Break down the note taking task by asking specific questions:
   (a) What questions you want to answer with this information?
   (b) Have you noted similar information already?
   (c) Any specific information? Names and dates?

4. Include references (page numbers, etc. for checking back)

CREATING MAP OF NOTES – MIND MAPS

In this stage of creative note taking, we write notes in radiant format by using symbols and images, wherever possible, along with the keywords. This technique is popularly known as **Mind Maps®**, invented by *Tony Buzan*.

It is a graphical technique that mirrors the way the brain works. The subject of interest is crystallized in a central image and then the main themes radiate out from the central image on branches. Each branch holds a key image or key word printed on the line. Details are added to the main branches and radiate out.

Most people's notes are on lined paper using blue or black ink which looks extremely boring. To make your notes more attractive to your brain, **add colour, rhythm, and imagination** and all of a sudden taking notes becomes much more fun.

Make creative notes for quick revision as explained in the chapter 'Mind Maps—Creative Note Taking'. Here is an example of creating a mind map® step-by-step for a given long answer:

Q. **What are the effects of the policy of Sri Lanka on Sri Lankan Tamils?**

Ans. The government measures, coming one after the other, gradually increased the feeling of alienation among the Sri Lankan Tamils. They felt that none of the major political parties led by the Buddhist Sinhala leaders were sensitive to their language and culture. They felt that the constitution and government policies denied them equal political rights, discriminated against them in getting jobs and other opportunities and ignored their interests. As a result, the relations between the Sinhala and Tamil communities strained over times. The Sri LankanTamils launched parties and struggled for the recognition of Tamil as an official language, for regional autonomy and equality of opportunity in securing education and jobs. But their demand was repeatedly denied. By the 1980s, several political organizations were formed demanding an independent Tamil Elam in northern and eastern parts of Sri Lanka. The distrust between twocommunities turned into widespread conflict. It soon turned into a civil war. As a result thousands of people of both the communities have been killed. Many families were forced to leave the country as refugees and many more lost their livelihoods.

To make a mind map of this answer, first convert this whole paragraph into points and then identify the key words from each point. Using those keywords, make a mind map systematically, putting along appropriate images as explained step by step in the next few pages:

Q. What are the effects of the policy of Sri Lanka?

Ans.:

    ❧ The **government measures**, coming one after the other, gradually **increased** the **feeling of alienation** among the Sri Lankan Tamils.

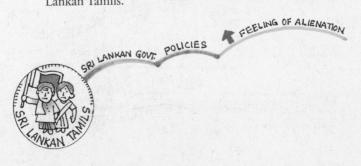

❖ They **felt** that **none** of the major **political parties** led by the Buddhist Sinhala leaders were **sensitive** to their **language** and **culture**.

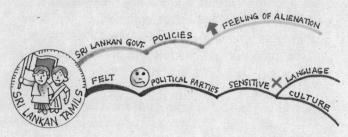

❖ They felt that the **constitution and government policies denied** them **equal political rights, discriminated** against them in getting **jobs** and other **opportunities** and ignored their interests.

❖ As a **result**, the **relations** between the Sinhala and Tamil communities **strained** over times.

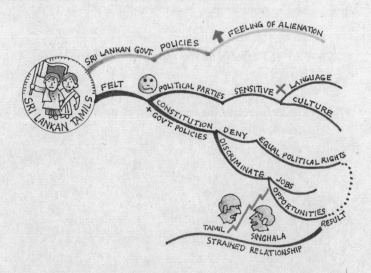

❖ The Sri Lankan Tamils **launched parties** and **struggled** for the recognition of **Tamil** as an **official language**, for **regional autonomy** and **equality** of **opportunity** in securing **education** and **jobs**. But their demand was repeatedly **denied**.

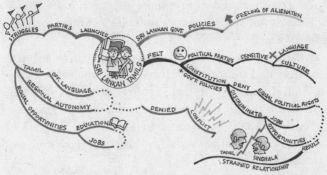

By the 1980s, several political organizations were formed demanding an independent Tamil Elam in northern and eastern parts of Sri Lanka. The distrust between two communities turned into widespread conflict. It soon turned into a **civil war**. As a result **thousands** of **people** of both the communities have been **killed**. Many **families** were forced to **leave** the country as **refugees** and many more **lost** their **livelihoods**.

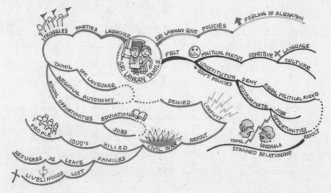

see appendix II 'mind maps' for colourful image of the above mind map

USE MEMORY TECHNIQUES

As students, we all have to remember a lot of theory and complex numerical data. Although some people might be good at mugging up, such practices yield no result in the long run. Instead if we convert this information into meaningful images, it will be easy to memorize it through associations and will stay with us for a longer period of time.

In the previous chapters we have learnt this art of using memory techniques through various methods. In the student section you will find various ways of applying these techniques in different areas of your course. Though the techniques and methods can be applied according to your ease and understanding, here is a brief summary of the methods with their suggested application in the table below:

S. NO.	MEMORY METHOD	APPLICATION
1.	Chain Method	Points in sequence, short answers in points, keywords of long answers, classifications, etc.
2.	Hide-and-Seek Method	Speech, points of presentations, list of words, answers in points, long answers in detail, etc.
3.	PNN (Personal Nick Name)	Scientific terminology, abstract information, vocabulary, foreign language, general knowledge facts, historical names, etc.
4.	Peg Method	Number sequences, constants, melting point, boiling point, periodic table, valancies, history dates, square roots, cube roots, etc.

| 5. | Acronyms | Long names, list or any collection of words, technical and scientific information (list of bones, nerves in medicine), etc. |
| 6. | Acrostics | Data of upto 10 words in specific order, trigonometry formula, taxonomy in biology, spellings, steps in a process, types of information, etc. |

SCIENTIFIC REVISION PLAN

WHY TO REVISE?

The revision period is, arguably, the most difficult part of any exam process, yet it is an important and unavoidable step.

Imagine you are passing through a dense forest. On the first day, the path is full of wild bushes and you find it extremely difficult to pass through. But instead of giving up, you clear the bushes and make a way to cross it. It was hard work and took a lot of time. But the next day, when you take the same route, it becomes a little easier as you push back more of the branches. Gradually, day by day, a clear path emerges.

Learning is a lot like that: **repetition gradually strengthens your memory pathways**. The more times you travel the same routes, the stronger the memory gets. If you only experience something once, and don't think about it again, it will almost certainly be forgotten.

WHEN TO REVISE?

Most information we take in through our senses is forgotten very quickly. There is a mechanism which must be activated if a memory is to go into a long-term store.

A nineteenth century German psychologist caller *Hermann Ebbinghaus* discovered that forgetting follows an exponential slope. In other words, the sharpest drop in our memory of something occurs nearest to the time we experience it, but then the drop off evens out.

This means that the first hours and days are the most important time for reviewing new information you want to remember in the long term. The younger a memory, the more vulnerable and weak it is.

Imagine each memory as a sick newborn kitten. If you can just nurse it through it's first 24 hours, then its chances of survival double. If you can nurse it through its first week, its chances double again, and after that it will only required attention now and then in order to survive.

If you think that once you are thorough with the concept, you can revise it only at the time of exam, you are highly mistaken. Look at the curve of forgetting given below.

CURVE OF FORGETTING

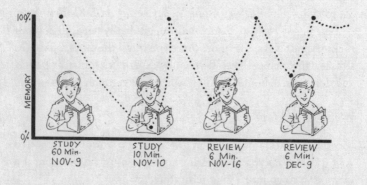

CURVE OF FORGETTING

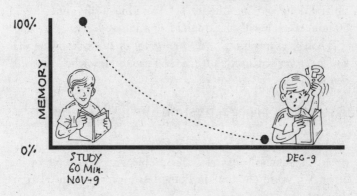

The graph above clearly shows that if you are revising something regularly, you **need just 5 minutes to refresh your memory after a month** to recall the details, whereas if you do not revise the topic, you will be completely blank when you will refer to it after a month.

Here is suggested schedule for reviewing information you want to store in long-term memory:

- ❖ one hour,
- ❖ one day,
- ❖ one week,
- ❖ one month,
- ❖ one season (three months)
- ❖ one year

Student may argue that revising a topic or chapter so many times is very time consuming and impractical. This may be because they read whole answers or chapters again and again from the book itself, whereas reading the whole chapter is required only in the beginning to understand. After that, if a student prepares notes by focusing on the keywords or important points from the subject matter, revising those notes becomes very easy.

Besides this, revision takes only 10 percent of the first learning time, if done within 24 hours, i.e. if you memorize something in 60 minutes, you will take around 5–6 minutes to revise the same.

Though exams bring with them a lot of stress, knowing that you have revised everything as planned brings relief and self-confidence.

BEWARE OF: PROCRASTINATION AND DISTRACTION

Procrastination is an act or a habit of putting off things for a later time. All human beings face this problem at some time or the other. We waste our time in doing less urgent tasks in place of urgent ones.

Today's age of high-end gadgets and technology plus exposure to 'n' number of means of entertainment adds to this habit. Once you switch on the *TV* to take a break of 15 minutes from your studies, you will not even realize that you spent an hour surfing on various channels, thus wasting your time and energy.

WhatsApp, Facebook, Hike and other similar social networking platforms give you an excuse to procrastinate your studies. No matter what time it is, replying to your friend's message seems more important than completing the topic at hand.

Every problem has a solution. This problem of procrastination can be solved in four simple yet important steps.

1. **Admit it:** Admit that you have a problem of procrastination, only then will you look for solutions.

2. **List:** Make a list of all the excuses you make to avoid doing work and then confront them with a positive mind.

EXCUSE	REALISTIC THOUGHT
The topic is too long. I will do it later.	I will divide the topic in parts and start by taking up one part at a time.
Right now is not the perfect time to start.	I feel so energetic that I feel this is the right time to start.
I will do it early morning.	I will finish it now so that I can sleep without any tension and start something fresh tomorrow morning.

3. **Affirmations:** Affirmations are positive thoughts that we should keep giving ourselves as motivation. Just admitting that you're lazy will not help. Give yourself affirmations such as: *'I know that I have the skills,* resources, and energy to get my to-do list done'.

'I choose to be a productive person.'
'I believe in the effort I make. I know that my work will generate results.'

4. **Accountability and reward:** When you have decided to do a task, you must also decide the result of not doing it as well as the reward for accomplishing it. For example, if you have planned to finish a chapter of Geography by 5 o'clock in the evening, plan how you will reward yourself if you are able to do it on time. You could reward yourself with a game of badminton with friends or a visit to a nearby market etc. Then you should also decide the result of not completing the task like missing the movie you planned to watch the next day or getting up one hour early to finish the topic etc.

Just make sure that the reward is motivating as well as realistic so that you feel like meeting the deadline.

EXAM TIPS: NO FEAR, NOW THAT EXAMS ARE HERE!

When you are preparing for an exam:

- ❖ Review all the new material daily and weekly.
- ❖ Understand the content fully instead of just memorizing it.
- ❖ Link new material to previously learned material.
- ❖ Frequently test yourself on your knowledge of the material.

One to two weeks before the exam:

- ❖ Prioritize your course material on the basis of previous exams or practice papers.
- ❖ Ask your teacher what the exam format will be (e.g. multiple choice, short answer).
- ❖ Do a 30-minute overview of each course.
- ❖ Create review tools such as checklists, summaries, flash cards, or mock exams.
- ❖ Plan a realistic schedule for each exam and prioritize according to the exam's weightage and difficulty, as well as how you are doing in the course.

Day(s) before the exam

- ❖ Check the location and time of the exam.
- ❖ Get adequate sleep and exercise.
- ❖ Limit coffee, alcohol, and caffeinated food/beverages.
- ❖ Eat well-balanced meals.
- ❖ Get all your exam tools ready the night before.
- ❖ Maintain a positive attitude.

Day of the exam

- Do not try to learn something new hours before the exam; in fact for most students, it is best not to study on the day of the exam.
- Be careful not to compare yourself to others or berate yourself for not studying more.
- If you feel overly anxious, take steps to relax yourself such as deep breathing or a brisk walk.
- Arrive early but not so early that you get anxious.
- Avoid talking to other students (anxiety spreads).
- Give yourself affirmations like, 'I know I can do it', 'I have studied well and will do well in exams'.
- Visualize yourself doing well in your exams with full confidence and belief.

These study skills will help you in the optimum utilization of your time, thereby yielding great results. If you keep following these skills, efficient time management will become a way of your life, which will be beneficial for you not only as a student but in the future as well.

PART D

TRICKS TO AMAZE YOUR FRIENDS

23

MEMORIZING 500-YEARS CALENDAR

Calendar plays an important role in our day-to-day life. Every now and then, we refer to a calendar, be it for planning an event or a program, fixing an appointment, going for a vacation, planning an exam schedule etc.

How would you feel if you could have the calendar for the next 500 years at your fingertips?

In my seminars, I ask a person from the audience about their birth *date*, and from that I'm instantly able to tell them the correct *day of the week* on which they were born and they just look at me unbelievably.

With the knowledge of *phonetic codes, shape peg codes,* and some *basic calculation*, you can also know the answer and surprise your friends and relatives by telling the day of the week they were born in less than 5 seconds. **Memorizing a calendar is very useful for competitive exams as well**, where questions related to dates and ages are asked.

It will allow you to amaze and impress your family and friends with seemingly impossible mental feats. It's actually quite easy to do with a little practice.

MEMORIZING 500 YEAR CALENDAR

If we observe any date, there are 4 main things:
- ✤ date,

❖ month,
❖ century, and
❖ year

We give each of these some particular codes. The sum of all these codes helps in determining the day of the week on which any given date falls.

Let's understand the process and memorize the codes:

CODES FOR DATE

Divide the date **by 7.**
Write the *remainder* as the code of the date.
Let's say the **date is 23,**
then $23 \div 7$ gives 2 as the remainder
So, the code for the date (23) is **2.**
If the **date is 6**, then $6 \div 7$ gives 6 as remainder
So, code for date (6) is **6.**

If the date is less than 7, then we can directly take the date as the remainder, as in the above case where the date is 6.

CODES FOR MONTHS

MONTH	CODE
January	1
February	4
March	4
April	0
May	2
June	5

MONTH	CODE
July	0
August	3
September	6
October	1
November	4
December	6

Table: 1

The month codes seem difficult to memorize as they don't follow any clear logic as seen in the table above. Now, here is an easy way to memorize these codes using some association as given in the chart below for your reference:

MONTH	CODE	ASSOCIATION
January	1	January is the 1st month of a year
February	4	Leap year comes in February every 4th year
March	4	March is immediately after February, so share the same code as February, i.e. 4
April	0	On April Fool's day we become 0 (fool) from hero
May	2	May reminds me of 2 options may be or may not be, so code is 2
June	5	Taking out Joo (lice) with the help of a hook (5)

MONTH	CODE	ASSOCIATION
July	0	July can be pronounced as ZOOly and big zeroes indicate the code 0
August	3	15th August (Independence Day) reminds us of National tri-coloured Flag, so code is 3
September	6	September starts with 'S' and Six also starts with 'S', so code is 6
October	1	October starts with 'O' and One also starts with 'O', so code is 1
November	4	'N' of November looks like Roman Numeral 4 (IV)
December	6	December sounds like Dice, which has 6 sides, so code is 6

Table: 2

CODES FOR CENTURIES

CENTURY	CODE
1600's	6
1700's	4
1800's	2
1900's	0
2000's	6
2100's	4

Table: 3

Observe that the pattern *6–4–2–0* goes on repeating in sequence again.

Code for current century 2000 = **6 or–1**

(Instead of adding 6 you can subtract 1 to simplify the calculation. It will give the same result.)

CODES FOR YEARS

YEAR	CODE	YEAR	CODE	YEAR	CODE	YEAR	CODE
01	1	26	4	51	0	76	4
02	2	27	5	52	2	77	5
03	3	28	0	53	3	78	6
04	5	29	1	54	4	79	0
05	6	30	2	55	5	80	2
06	0	31	3	56	0	81	3
07	1	32	5	57	1	82	4
08	3	33	6	58	2	83	5
09	4	34	0	59	3	84	0
10	5	35	1	60	5	85	1
11	6	36	3	61	6	86	2
12	1	37	4	62	0	87	3
13	2	38	5	63	1	88	5
14	3	39	6	64	3	89	6
15	4	40	1	65	4	90	0
16	6	41	2	66	5	91	1
17	0	42	3	67	6	92	3
18	1	43	4	68	1	93	4
19	2	44	6	69	2	94	5

YEAR	CODE	YEAR	CODE	YEAR	CODE	YEAR	CODE
20	4	45	0	70	3	95	6
21	5	46	1	71	4	96	1
22	6	47	2	72	6	97	2
23	0	48	4	73	0	98	3
24	2	49	5	74	1	99	4
25	3	50	6	75	2		

Table: 4

Example 1:

Now, let's take the date **23rd May, 1992**

Date = **23** ÷ 7 gives *Remainder* = **2**
Month = May = **2** *(ref. table 1)*
1992 = 0 + 3 = **3** *(ref. table 3 and 4)*

Date	Month	Century	Year
2	2	0	3

Adding all the codes together, we get:
2 + 2 + 0 + 3 = 7

This final sum 7 will tell the day of the week. Each day has its own code as shown in the table below:

CODES FOR DAYS

DAY	CODE
Sunday	1
Monday	2
Tuesday	3
Wednesday	4
Thursday	5
Friday	6
Saturday	7 or 0

Table: 5

Since 7 corresponds to Saturday, so the day on 23rd May, 1992 was **Saturday**.

MEMORIZING CODES OF THE YEAR

Memorizing specific codes for 100 years in a century is very confusing. You can memorize them if we can convert both the years and their respective codes into images and then make some association between the two. The years from 01 to 99 can be given images using the phonetic peg system.

As the codes for the years range from 0 to 6 only, these codes can be converted into images with the use of the shape method as shown below:

Codes	Shape pegs
0	Egg
1	Candle
2	Duck
3	Heart

Codes	Shape pegs
4	Chair
5	Hook
6	Hockey Stick

Let's say the code for **92** is **3**.
Phonetic Peg for year 92—BuN
Shape peg for code 3—Heart
Association: Visualize heart-shaped buns.

Similarly, the code for **year 15** is **4**.
Phonetic Peg for year 15—Doll
Shape peg for code 4—Chair
Association—Visualize a Doll is dancing on a Chair.

In the same way, you can make association between all the 100 years and their respective codes.

Some more examples:
Find days of the week on which of the following dates fall:

Example 2:

28th March, 1980
    Date = 28 ÷ 7 gives Remainder = 0
    Month = March = 4 *(ref. table 1)*
    1980 = 0 + 2 = 2 *(ref. table 3 and 4)*
    Adding all, we get 0 + 4 + 2 = 6.
    6 is the code corresponding to Friday.

So, 28th March, 1980 was a **Friday**.

Example 3:

5th April, 2010
   Date = 5 ÷ 7 gives Remainder = 5
   Month = April = 0
   Year = 2010 = 6 + 5 = 11
   Total = 5 + 0 + 11 = 16,
   Again 16 ÷ 7 gives the remainder = 2

2 stands for **Monday**.

> Note: When the final total is more than 7, divide it again
> by 7 and the remainder thus obtained corresponds to
> the code of the day.

IN CASE OF LEAP YEAR

If the given year is a **leap year** and the months are **January or February**, then reduce 1 day from the day calculated.

Example 4:

   23rd Feb., 1976
   2 + 4 + 0 + 4 = 10
   10 ÷ 7 gives remainder as 3 and 3 stands for Tuesday.

Ideally the day should be Tuesday, but 1976 is a leap year, so as per the rule for calculating the day in the leap year, we reduce one day, i.e. instead of Tuesday, the day would be Monday.

So, 23rd Feb, 1976 was a **Monday**.

How Do You Know It's a Leap Year?

As soon as you hear the months of January and February, immediately check if it is a leap year (*if the given year is divisible by 4, it means it's a leap year*). If it is, then reduce one day from the day calculated.

If the year is leap year but the months are from March to December, then there is no need for any adjustment. We make adjustment only in the months of January and February.

With practice, you can tell the day of any date within 5 seconds.

Try finding out day of the following dates:

(1) 8th Nov., 1956
(2) 19th Nov., 2005
(3) 2nd Oct., 1869
(4) 3rd Jan., 1984
(5) 7th April, 2008

24

MEMORIZING LONG SERIES OF NUMBERS

In this chapter, we are going to share an amazing secret that will enable you to be a star among your family and friends. It is a game of numbers we play in most of our seminars. We ask the audience to give us random numbers *(say about 100 numbers)* that we note down on a board. Immediately after that we recall the whole sequence of those numbers with our eyes closed. We even tell the numbers in reverse order. The audience usually breaks into an impromptu applause, amazed at our feat.

Let us share the secret of doing that with you.

Suppose this is the list of numbers you have to memorize:

923456599126788505481953989572

You might think that memorizing such a long number will take time but it's really very easy.

- ❖ Break the above sequence of numbers in 15 pairs of 2-digit each. Use phonetic method to convert them into words.
- ❖ Now, memorize these 15 words in a sequence using chain method or hide-and-seek method.

Let's understand it by following the given steps:

Step 1:

Break the long series into pairs of 2 digits

| 92 | 34 | 56 | 59 | 91 | 26 | 78 | 85 |
| 05 | 48 | 19 | 53 | 98 | 95 | 72 | |

Step 2:

Decode the pairs with the help of phonetic peg codes
(as done in chapter 13, using the advance peg system)

92	BuN
34	aMiR
56	LeeCH
59	LaB
91	BaT
26	NehRu
78	KoFee
85	FiLe
05	SaLe
48	RooF
19	TaP
53	LiMe
98	B.F.
95	BelL
72	KoNe

Thus to memorize a sequence of 30 digits in a series, you have to memorize only 15 words.

These words can be memorized in a sequence using:

(a) Chain Method

(b) Hide-and-Seek Method

Step 3:

(a) Memorizing using Chain Method

Visualization:

Visualize that there are lots of *buns*. *Amir Khan* comes and starts eating them. All of a sudden, a big *leech* comes out of his mouth. The leech is taken to a *lab* to experiment. The lab is full of *bats*. One bat is gifted to *Nehruji*. He starts drinking the *coffee*. The coffee alls on the *file*. The file is put on *sale*. While the sale was going on, the *roof* collapsed. *A tap* was opened to wash everything but instead of water, *lime* water started coming out. I gave this limewater to my *best friend (B.F.)*, who was holding a gigantic *bell*. Inside the bell, there were lots of *cones*.

Now repeat this visualization in your mind and try to recall the words you have memorized. And write them in sequence in the space given below:

1. _____buns_____	2. _____
3. _____	4. _____
5. _____	6. _____
7. _____	8. _____
9. _____	10. _____
11. _____	12. _____
13. _____	14. _____
15. _____	

Now, while visualizing the words in your mind, try to decode these words by their respective numbers: _____
_____
_____

(b) Memorizing using Hide-and-Seek method

After decoding the numbers into words or images in step 2 above, now recall the list of your hiding places created in the 'hide-and-seek method' chapter. Then associate each word with the hiding locations one by one in a sequence.

After all the images have been associated with their respective hiding places, visualize the stops in a sequence and try to decode each associated word into number as you move on in your journey.

> Tip: You may recall the sequence in the reverse order as well just by visualizing your hiding places starting from the end and moving one place backwards each time, during your recall.

With practice, you will soon be able to directly decode the word images into numbers as you visualize your associations in mind.

APPLYING MEMORY TRICKS TO YOUR WORKING LIFE

You may argue what's the need to memorize 30 random number sequences or what's the use of mastering calendar of 500 years when a calendar can be accessed on a mobile also?

These memory stunts not only help you amaze your friends and family and become a hero in front of them, they will also motivate you to apply these methods in your day-to-day life and increase your self-confidence. For example, the calendar trick can be used to **plan your events in the future** and check if that falls on a specific day or on a weekend. Similarly, memorizing a list of long numbers can be helpful in **remembering credit card numbers** (16 digits) or bank account numbers or any other numerical data.

Also, these activities are a good workout for your brain and help you improve your concentration as well. They are the practical application of the methods learnt in the previous chapters. Once you start practicing these activities, *your mind will be conditioned to memorize information automatically using these methods instead of depending on latest gadgets.*

So what are you waiting for? Prepare yourself to earn the title of *'Memory King'* or *'Memory Queen'* from your peers.

25

MEMORIZING PLAYING CARDS

Playing cards offer much more than an amusing pastime. They can be used for endlessly fascinating memory practice. You can learn to memorize a complete deck of 52 cards and amaze your friends with this memory stunt.

Cards are, by their very nature, difficult to memorize, in much the same way as numbers are. To memorize a deck of 52 cards in a sequence, we need a system for **assigning a particular word and image to each card**, thereby immediately making them more individual, more tangible, and more memorable.

There are different ways to do this, and you shouldn't think that you have to do it in a certain way only:

- ❧ King of Hearts could be your dad.
- ❧ Queen of Hearts could be your mom.
- ❧ 5 of Hearts could be your daughter Sharon because she is 5-years-old and you love her *(hearts could mean love for you)*.
- ❧ Jack of Hearts could be a Joker holding a big heart.
- ❧ Ace of Clubs can be visualized as a big tree.
- ❧ Four Jacks could be four top sports stars.
- ❧ Four Queens could be four top actresses as the queens.
- ❧ Four Kings could be four former presidents.

- The Jack, Queen, and King of each suit can be personalities from different fields.
- Shape of Nine of Diamonds looks like H, which can further be visualized as Harry Potter.

There are advantages of this method, but to make things a bit easier, instead of memorizing 52 new peg words, you can use a bunch of the peg words you have already memorized for 0 to 99.

Although the choice of peg words depends on you, here we are sharing with you the words and images that we have assigned to 52 cards.

MEMORY PEGS FOR CARDS: ACE TO 10

For each card, one word is assigned. That word comprises two parts:

- The first part represent the first letter of the suit:

  C for *Clubs*♣,

  H for *Hearts*♥,

  S for *Spades*♠, and

  D for *Diamonds*♦

- The second part of the word represents the *phonetic peg* given to the value of card.

Example 1:

If the card is **6 of clubs** (C6) then it will be represented by the word **Cash**, where:

- *C* corresponds to *clubs* and
- *sh* corresponds to 6 *(according to the phonetic peg system)*.

Example 2:

Similarly, **2 of Diamonds** (D2) can be given the word **Den**, where:

- ✤ *D* corresponding to *Diamonds* and
- ✤ *2* corresponding to *n* (phonetic peg system)

Example 3:

For **Hearts**, the first letter is *H*, so **H1** *(Ace of Hearts)* can be assigned the word **Hat**.

Similarly *2 of Hearts*, **H2** corresponds to **Hen** and so on.

MEMORY PEGS FOR: JACKS

For all four Jacks, I visualize the original suits only.

- ✤ Jack of Clubs can be seen as a **golf club**,
- ✤ Jack of Hearts can be seen as a **heart**,
- ✤ Jack of Spade can be seen as a **spade**, and
- ✤ Jack of Diamonds can be seen as a **diamond**.

MEMORY PEGS FOR: KING AND QUEEN

For images of King and Queen, I use Bollywood stars from romantic films for the hearts suit, sport stars for clubs, politicians for spades, and rich individuals for diamonds.

> *It doesn't really matter what image you are giving to a card.*
> *What matters is that you remember which image is*
> *for which card!*

*As long as you can give each playing card an identity,
it becomes memorable.*

Here's a list of all the card words we use for all four suits.
*(Although these are only suggestions and it's recommended that you use
your own images).*

Memorize playing cards with these words and images:

	♣ Clubs	♥ Hearts	♠ Spades	♦ Diamonds
Ace	Cat	Hat	Suit	Dad
2	Cone	Honey	Sun	Den
3	Comb	Home	Sumo	Dam
4	Car	Hare/Hair	Sir	Dr.
5	Coal	Hall	Sale	Doll
6	Cash	Hedge	Sage	Dish
7	Cake	Hook	Sky	Deck
8	Coffee	Hive	Sofa	Dwarf
9	Cap	Hoop	Soap	Dope
10	Case	Hose	Sause	Dosa
Jack	Club	Heart	Spade	Diamond
Queen	Mary Kom	Aishwarya Rai	Sonia Gandhi	Queen Elizabeth
King	Sachin Tendulkar	Shahrukh Khan (King Khan)	Narendra Modi	Bill Gates

Once you have successfully created images for the cards in your
mind, you'll be able to associate them to *anything*—to each other
by the chain method (to remember a sequence), or to hiding places
(to remember them in and out of order), or to anything else.

The important thing here is to get into the habit of seeing the image, not just knowing the word. When you see the 5 of Diamonds, you should almost immediately see a mental image of a **doll**. For the 6 of Spades, a **sage**. For the 2 of Clubs, a **cone**. It's important to 'see' these mental images and not just be aware of the words.

There is no rhyme or reason as to where these pictures come from and it doesn't matter. All that matters is that you:

1. *Create the images that make sense to YOU.*
2. *Spend time looking through a deck of cards over and over and over until you can recognize the image that goes with the card without hesitation.*
3. *Using chain or hide-and-seek method, memorize the whole sequence.*

This practice of memorizing the sequence of 52 cards is beneficial in many ways:

1. It's an amazing way to *master your memory skills* so that you can use it easily in your day-to-day life.
2. You can play some very interesting memory games and *impress your friends*.
3. One of the most important aspects of memory is actually focusing your attention on the subject matter, and this method *forces you to focus*.

The mental exercise your brain will be undergoing, creating all those fascinating mental images and scenarios, is absolutely invaluable. Learning how to memorize playing cards is one of the most challenging and most satisfying tests of mental agility that you could undertake.

Appendix I

FREQUENTLY ASKED QUESTIONS

Q1. Will my memory decline with age?

Ans. There is no reason that your memory will decline with age unless you're suffering from some medical illness. In fact, your ability to learn and remember should get better as you get older. Different memory techniques use the information you already know to form new memories. The older you get, the more you know, the more experiences you will have, and the more you will be able to learn. Many people feel that their memory is becoming weak, but this is not because they are ageing. The actual reason is that they have stopped using it as much as they used to earlier. Another reason for the apparent decline in performance of memory as we grow older is that we become physically less active, and therefore our brain gets less oxygen than it used to.

Q2. **Is it possible to improve my memory?**

Ans. Absolutely! The techniques of memory improvement have existed for thousands of years and are helping major firms today. These techniques have proven to be useful for people from all walks of life like scholars, businessmen, doctors, lawyers, students, housewives etc.

Q3. **Is modern technology (computers, smartphones, tablets, PCs etc.) a good substitute for memory?**

Ans. Day-by-day, our dependency on gadgets and new technology is increasing. Though modern technology helps us access any information at our fingertips, the greatest drawback of increased use of these gadgets is that we have stopped using our own brains even for small things. Don't you think that it would be better if you could tell the details of a project to a client directly instead of asking him to wait a minute till you check it on your smartphone. These gadgets are good as backups, but being totally dependent on them may have a harmful effect on the ability to use your brain.

Q4. **Isn't it easier to memorize material directly, instead of using these memory techniques?**

Ans. Memory systems may appear complex at first, but once you're familiar with them, their time and energy saving value is more than apparent. In fact, these techniques can help you save time in revision and you will be able to recall quickly and retain information for a longer period of time easily. The tedious task of memorizing by rote requires you to repeat the material to yourself 8 to 10 times before anything starts to stick. And there's no guarantee it will stay with you for a long period of time.

For example: If you want to put anything in your cupboard, there are two ways to do it. One is to keep stacking all things one over the other and the second is to demarcate separate spaces for daily wear clothes, books, cosmetics, footwear, party dresses etc. Don't you think it is easier to find a thing in the second case? Similarly, our brain is also like a cupboard. We will be able to access the things we have remembered much better if we put them in a systematic way.

Q5. **I am not able to make ridiculous visualizations. Is it okay if I make simple associations without much detail?**

Ans. It's absolutely okay if your visualizations are simple. It hardly matters what you visualize as far as it is helping you to remember. The reason I suggest you to make ridiculous visualizations is that it will stand out when you are trying to recall. For example, in your shopping list if you are trying to memorize tomatoes, you should imagine them as huge and bright red in colour. This way they will stand out and will immediately come to your mind. Initially you might find it a little difficult to make funny images but with time and practice you will certainly be able to do so.

Q6. **Can memory systems help with corporate training?**

Ans. Now-a-days it has become a trend in big companies to make employees go through various forms of training just to score on employee satisfaction whereas it is quite evident that hardly any of these trainings help them in the long run. The reason is that after a period of time, most employees remember only that part of training they apply to their current job. The rest of it goes waste. Memory skills should be the first thing we all should learn so that whatever we learn afterwards stays with us for a long time. These techniques help you in all spheres of life—be it studies, work, or day-to-day activities.

Q7. **Why do people today have such a bad memory?**

Ans. In the beginning of the book, I had mentioned that there is no such thing as bad memory. Your memory is either trained or untrained. Whenever we forget some basic information, we start doubting our memory. But it's not that simple; there are various factors affecting our retention and recall powers. These factors have been discussed in details in the chapter 'Techniques to Improve Concentration'. Generally speaking, our lifestyle is mainly responsible for this problem. We are much too dependent on the latest gadgets and techniques and don't use our brain even for simple things. Physical activity is decreasing at an alarming rate with every generation. The same is the case with mental activity.

Puzzles, mental games, meditation, and various other activities can help in enhancing the powers of the brain.

Q8. **Do memory techniques help in making money?**

Ans. *'Time is money.' 'A penny saved is a penny earned.'*

These popular sayings show you the importance of saving time. Memory system aims to do that and much more. Here is a short list of some of the concrete examples of where memory systems can make or save money:

- Without memory aids, an executive spends 30 minutes a day looking for things on his desk.
- As you will be able to remember all the points discussed in a meeting, even if it was an informal one, it will create a positive impression on the client or the other party.

❖ Having information on your fingertips instead of your gadgets increases you credibility thus resulting in better business.

❖ It results in better relations with clients by recalling more about them.

❖ It helps in strengthening relationships with your employer as well as employees, thus enhancing productivity.

Q9. **I feel confused about which memory technique to apply in which situation. What if I learn only one method and apply it in all scenarios?**

Ans. When you learn something new, it always seems complex in the beginning. But with practice, you gain expertise in the same area. The same is the case with memory techniques. You might find one method easy and another one difficult, but if you give it time, you can be a pro in all methods and will enjoy them even more. Once you start using these techniques in various fields or subjects, you will be able to decide which method works in which situation. When you think of making a delicious dish, you have to use many ingredients as each ingredient has a unique and special quality. Similarly each memory technique has its own unique utility. Generally when you have to memorize a data in points, the chain or hide-and-seek method is suitable. For numerical information, pegs are most appropriate. But you will notice that many a time only one method is not enough and you will have to use a combination of memory techniques to memorize the given information.

Q10. **In the hide-and-seek method, is it okay if I remember all information using only one route?**

Ans. It is not advisable to use a single route or location every time because it will lead to confusion. A single thing or location will remind you of many things that you have associated with it. It's better to use a different setting to memorize different information. But if you are remembering things like shopping lists or points of speech or a number sequence, where information is not actually required after the work has been done, you can use the same location. Your brain can hold information for only a few hours if you don't constantly rehearse your images or associations. So it will automatically help you delete the old information and save the new one on that route or location.

Q11. **When associating information to facial features, what if I find it difficult to notice anything unusual in the person's face?**

Ans. When we look at somebody for the first time, there is always something in his/her appearance that attracts attention. You have to be a little attentive to find that detail. But if you are not able to find something unusual or distinctive, put your imagination at work. Try and enhance the features a little more in your mind and then associate the information.

Q12. **Is it not risky to associate information to someone's hair as one might change one's hairstyle?**

Ans. When you are linking some information to a person's hair, it is advisable to link it to the texture of the hair rather than the hairstyle. For example, a person having curly hair can change his hairstyle but the texture of hair will remain curly. Or a bald person, in all possibility, will remain bald. So you can easily use this feature to memorize his name.

Q13. **I work as a translator at an embassy and need to remember what is being said as I translate. Can you help?**

Ans. I would suggest that you only try and remember key words as someone speaks. For example: 'Sir, last Monday I was travelling from Delhi to Agra by train with three of my friends when I realized that my passport had been stolen. Although I reported the matter at the Agra station, I have not received a reply from them.' Out of these lines if you were to remember only key words, you could pick 'Agra to Delhi', 'train', 'Passport stolen', 'reported'. Now you just have to remember these four words and the related information will come to your mind when you mention them. Along with remembering only key words, I would suggest you to take notes using a mind map instead of conventional notes.

Q14. **Can we make world record using these techniques?**

Ans. Yes, in fact many of our students have made national records and world records. Many of them got their names registered in the **India book of Records** as Mind Masters.

Q15. **Does 'photographic memory' exist?**

Ans. Wow! Having a photographic memory sounds great. Imagine you simply look at a page from a book and then perfectly reproduce an image of that page in your mind.

But the bad news is that photographic memory has never been proven to exist. Scientists have done many experiments to prove this and have found that it's impossible to recall images with perfect accuracy. Some people do have phenomenal memories but they cannot be excellent in all areas. A chess master may beat multiple opponents but he may be bad at remembering birthdays and anniversaries.

But there are some exceptions. A few autistic people might have something close to this kind of memory. For example, 'Kim Peek' from America has memorized almost 12,000 books and only takes 8–10 seconds to memorize each page. The character Raymond Babbitt played by Dustin Hoffman in the film *Rain Man* is inspired by him.

Q16. **Do you think supplements can help me boost my memory?**

Ans. Today the market is full of medicines and other supplements that claim to increase your memory, but there are no studies to prove the same. Physical and mental exercise along with a proper and healthy diet is a more powerful way to boost your memory, even in old age. But sometimes a lack of some minerals in your body might affect your brain function and your doctor might prescribe some dietary supplements for it. Taking these will help prevent memory problems. Currently there is no proof that these supplements help in normal cases. People suffering from dementia are advised to follow the doctor's advice, as these are a different type of drug, necessary to take in such cases.

Q17. **Will these memory techniques work for me if I suffer from Dyslexia?**

Ans. As human beings, it's not natural for our brain to process and store information in the form of words or numbers. And the reason is because our brain is hard-wired to process information in the form of **mental images**.

This is one of the reasons why many people struggle with Dyslexia. The challenge, of course, is that we live in a world full of words and numbers. To help overcome this challenge, in this book you'll discover a system of techniques that will show you how to translate linguistic and numerical information into visual, mental images—tightly organized in your mind.

If you suffer from Dyslexia, the techniques taught in this book will help you take advantage of your brain's naturally strong ability for mental images, overcome challenges you might have with words and numbers, and dramatically improve your memory in the process.

Q18. I don't want to rely only on my memory to store my passwords. How can I create a secure backup for the same?

Ans. Almost all internet sites give you the option of resetting your password in case you forget it. However, you can create a back up for these by associating them with images or a series of sketches in your diary. These images will remind you about the associations you created with them and will be difficult for others to decode, thus ensuring security.

Q19. According to you, what is a better option for keeping my brain active in old age? Paper-based puzzles or online/video-based games?

Ans. There is no evidence to prove which is a better way of exercising your brain. It is entirely a matter of personal choice as to what challenges you want to do: puzzles and games in books or newspapers, or online games.

Q20. If I am confident that I understood the information correctly, do I need to still revise it?

Ans. In our daily life we absorb a lot of information, but can you recall all the information that you learnt in the past? No. Only if you revise what you have learnt or you associate some new information to an already existing one that you will be able to recall it whenever you need it. That makes revision very important.

Q21. Many a times I review a material but still forget it. What should I do about it?

Ans. First of all you have to identify the main problem. Ask yourself:
- Did you understand the information correctly in the first place?
- Did you encode it using correct memory techniques?

If the answer to the above question is yes, then you must consider how often are you reviewing this information? It might be possible that you are giving too much gap in revision or you are not concentrating on it completely while revising. Even if you have to understand the topic again, don't hesitate. Or you can change the memory technique that you were using to memorize it. Analyze all these aspects and then rectify the problem.

Q22.   **I have become so absentminded that I keep misplacing my books and notebooks. Sometimes I even forget in which book did I note down an important note. Please help.**

Ans.   Everything needs a place. You must create a separate place for your notebooks so that you know where to keep it and can easily find it when needed. To make it more easily accessible, you can code it by using different colour papers for different subjects. You can also create an index in each of the notebooks which will make it easy for you to access the topics you noted down in each notebook.

Q23.   **Does our emotional state effect out ability to memorize? I am a pessimist and most of the time I am in a negative state of mind. What should I do?**

Ans.   Yes. Our emotions play a very important role in the functioning of our brain. If we are anxious or worried, all our attention goes to those thoughts and it become difficult for us to concentrate on other things. If you are worried about something, face it and calm yourself down. Only then move on to learn something.

Q24   **I am a pessimist, so even though I try hard to stay positive, I tend to start thinking about negative experiences that further makes me remember other negative memories. What can I do about this?**

Ans.   Make an effort to improve your mood and recall happy memories. Put up photos of happy occasions in your working environment so you will see them during the day.

Q25.   Are there any other ways I can improve how I feel in everyday life?

Ans.   People definitely differ in their general levels of happiness, and this seems to be more due to genetics than to their situation in life. However, there are a few things you can do to improve your general mood:

- ❖ Get regular exercise
- ❖ Don't compare yourself too much with others and
- ❖ Don't always take failures personally
- ❖ Meditate

Q26.   Drawing even a simple straight line is a big task for me. Can I still use a mind map to memorize?

Ans.   Of course you can! Mind map is not a means to showcase your drawing talent. Your map need not have straight lines. It can have curved lines as long as it is drawn by you. The idea is to covert your notes into images so that it is easy to recall. So go ahead and enjoy converting long boring notes into amazing colourful mind maps.

Q27.   Is there any software available online to create mind maps?

Ans.   Yes. There is a lot of software available online and I have used a few but I found drawing on paper to be most effective. Working with mouse and keyboard may be less free flowing than doing it on paper, unless you have really good touch screens that allow you to write on the computer free hand.

Q28.   Do you recommend any memory training games available on internet?

Ans . Well, there is a lack of strong evidence that such games boost your memory but there may be some other benefits like increasing concentration or motivating you to pay more attention, which may in turn improve your memory. This is due to your increased attention to your work at hand, but there is no proof as such that these exercises can increase your ability to learn or recall other information also.

Q29. If I am speaking to someone on the phone, like a new client, how can I remember his name without meeting him face-to-face?

Ans. It is easier to remember the names in such a case because while you are speaking on the phone, you can note down their name straightaway. Then you can associate it directly with the matter of discussion or with their voice rather than the face. Concentrate on the texture of the voice like husky, sweet, sharp, loud etc. or his accent.

Q30. My work requires me to meet new people every now and then. I tried remembering their names by turning it in to a visual image but found it a little difficult and time consuming. What should I do?

Ans. 'Practice makes a man perfect.' Although in the beginning you may find it difficult, it will become a habit if you practice it regularly. You can start with your phone book and rehearse the names from it or try remembering names of people where it is not necessary to remember so that you are not under any pressure, like some salesperson at a departmental store *(seeing their name badges)*.

ACKNOWLEDGEMENTS

We would firstly like to thank the Almighty God for empowering us with the intellect and belief to write this book.

To our parents, for their unconditional support and for being a pillar of strength throughout our lives. Their encouraging words helped us to think and aim high and achieve success in life.

To B.K. Chakradhari didiji, who has always been a source of inspiration. She helped us in discovering our inner strengths by her ever encouraging words of knowledge and wisdom.

To Dr Biswaroop Roy Choudhary, for introducing us to this wonderful world of memory and for always being there as a friend, mentor and motivator.

To BK Chandra Shekhar Tiwari, for motivating us and for believing in our potential much before we started believing in ourselves.

Our sincere gratitude to Mr Bala Kishore, for taking special interest in the making of this book and for his valuable scientific inputs inspite of his extremely busy schedule.

To Mr M. Saquib, who worked very hard in bringing our imagination into the real world through his wonderful speaking illustrations for the book.

To our friend Jaya Kalwani, for taking keen interest and enthusiasm in making of this book. Because of your constant feedback, valuable inputs, and unbiased opinion we were able to make this book simple and interesting for all the readers.

To our students and their parents for believing in us. It is only because of our experience with our wonderful students that we are able to present these concepts in the simplest manner. Their persistent questions helped us to come up with various examples straight from their curriculum.

Special thanks to thousands of teachers from schools across the country who attended our training sessions. Their wonderful feedback about these amazing techniques inspired us to come out with this book.

To our sons, Devansh and Ishaan, the light of our life, who gave us a lot of insight as a student which immensely helped in teaching these techniques to other students.

To Milee Ashwarya and the complete editorial team of Random House India, for their efforts in the excellent publication of this book.

Finally, thank you to anyone whose names we may have missed out, but who have lent their support in any way to the book.

A NOTE ON THE AUTHORS

Aditi Singhal is an international memory trainer, author, motivational speaker, counsellor, and Vedic Math expert par excellence. She has to her credit the *Guinness World Record* for conducting the largest Maths class and three national records for memory and fastest calculation awarded by the *Limca Book of Records*. She has also been given 'The Best Memory Trainer' award by the *India Book of Records*. Her dream to make calculations simple for all resulted in the bestselling book *How to Become a Human Calculator?*
Email: mvedica@gmail.com
Website: www.aditisinghal.com

Sudhir Singhal is a dynamic trainer, author, motivational speaker and counsellor. He has to his credit the *Guinness World Record* for conducting the largest Maths class and a world record in the *Limca Book of Records*. He has been a source of inspiration for many youngsters. He has over fifteen years' experience in different fields like technology, programming, management, and education.
Email: sudhir.dmg@gmail.com

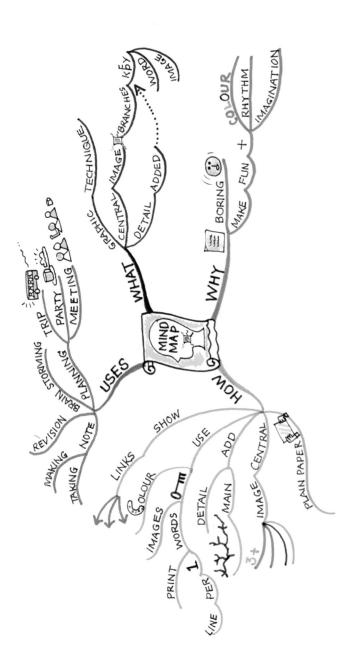

MIND MAP ABOUT THE CONCEPT OF MIND MAPPING

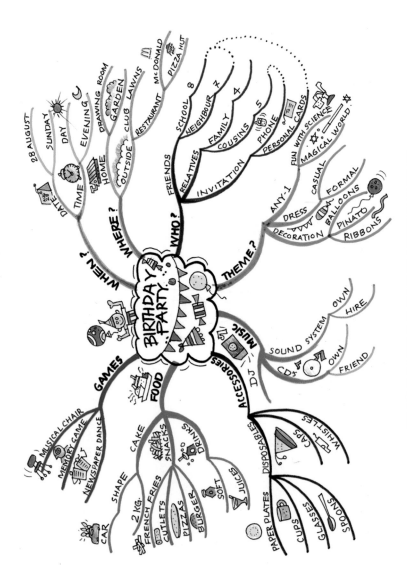

MIND MAP ABOUT PLANNING A BIRTHDAY PARTY

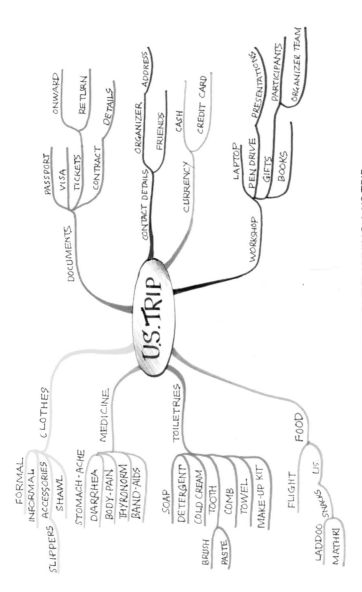

MIND MAP ABOUT PLANNING A US TRIP

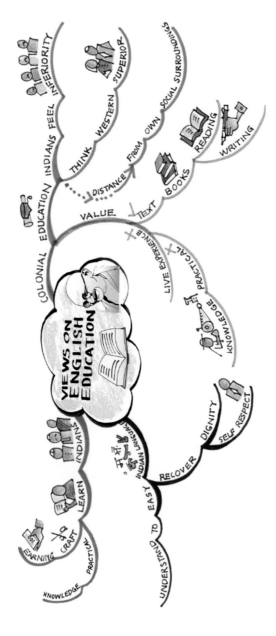

MIND MAP ABOUT THE VIEWS OF GANDHIJI ON ENGLISH EDUCATION

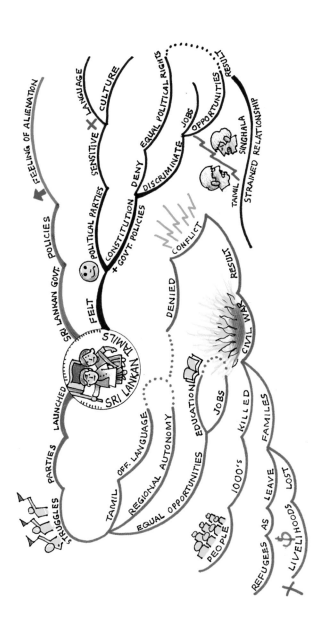

MIND MAP ABOUT THE EFFECTS OF THE POLICY OF SRI LANKA ON SRI LANKAN TAMILS

MIND MAP ABOUT HOW TO IMPROVE CONCENTRATION

CERTIFICATE

The largest maths class involved
2,312 participants and was achieved
by Aditi Singhal and Sudhir Singhal,
organized by Brahma Kumaris
(all India), in Gurgaon, Haryana, India,
on 17 December 2012

GUINNESS WORLD RECORDS

india
Book of Records
(Guinness World Record Holder's Enterprise)

CERTIFICATE

HONOR OF EXCELLENCE

**Aditi Singhal of Delhi is awarded with the
Memory Trainer's award 2009, for her
contribution in the field of Memory Training.**

Biswaroop Roy Chowdhury
Chief Editor
India Book of Records

Date:16 August 2009   INDIA BOOK OF RECORDS   www.asiabookofrecords.com

Limca

Book of Records

National Record 2010

Aditi Singhal (b Feb 23, 1976) of Delhi wrote down a 13-digit table in 1 min 13 sec in front of Limca Book of Records team members on August 30, 2010.

Vijaya Ghose
Editor, Limca Book of Records

Limca

Book of Records

National Record 2010

Aditi Singhal (b Feb 23, 1976) of Civil Lines, Delhi memorized 210 binary digits and recalled them with 100% accuracy at in 2 min 26 sec Limca Book of Records office, Gurgaon, Haryana on August 30, 2010.

Vijaya Ghose
Editor, Limca Book of Records